In Praise of
Fighting for the Progressive Center in the Age of Trump

"Joe Hoeffel is the genuine article. He's run for and held public office, at the county and country levels. He's won and lost elections. He's dealt with the real voters with real problems. He knows what matters to people. His voice comes from forty years dealing with people's real, kitchen-table politics. As someone who grew up and went to school near him, I know these challenges. People don't have time for all the polarization and demonization out there today. No one enjoys watching the rough-and-tumble of politics more than I do, but the time has come for political parties to get serious. Joe Hoeffel's book shows that he's way ahead of them. If the Democrats are smart they'll read this book."

—Chris Matthews, Anchor of MSNBC's *Hardball*

"When I joined the Congress in 2001, Joe Hoeffel stood out as a thoughtful, insightful Democrat, with a rare gift for communicating smart, progressive policies, and the even rarer gift of knowing how to win in the toughest districts. His newest book, *Fighting for the Progressive Center in the Age of Trump*, finds him as politically astute as ever, making the case for a 'progressive center' focused on improving the quality of life for all Americans. As Democrats move forward from the disaster of the 2016 election, Joe makes a timely case for policies and a message that can rise above our broken politics and get down to the business of governing."

—Adam B. Schiff, U.S. Congressman from California

"My good friend Joe Hoeffel has dedicated his life to public service and this book encapsulates his lessons for a Trump-era America. It is imperative that our country comes together to solve the challenges that we encounter in our daily lives. To truly make America even greater, Joe has put forward an agenda that is progressive and prioritizes jobs, health care, and a better quality of life for our hardworking families. We miss Joe on Capitol Hill, but this book makes clear that his leadership to Pennsylvania and America is far from finished."

—Edward Markey, U.S. Senator from Massachusetts

"Our country is divided more than ever. Yet, at the end of the day, most Americans want the same things—a good job, affordable health care for their families, retirement security, and opportunities for their children. Joe Hoeffel understands we have more in common than we have differences. *Fighting for the Progressive Center* speaks to what Americans want from government, and offers prescriptions for the pressing issues of the day—health care, economic development, Social Security, education reform."

—Tom Udall, U.S. Senator from New Mexico

"Hoeffel puts into words what so many of us wished for last election day—the requirements for a progressive candidate we could vote for. This books outlines how government has a valuable role to play in our society without dominating society, how our compassion towards each other, expressed through single-payer health care and a social safety net, is the answer America needs, not simple appeals to ideology and party memes."

—Peter Van Buren, Author, *Ghosts of Tom Joad:*
A Story of the 99 Percent

"Joe Hoeffel's book speaks to America's character when 'We the People' are at our best: the individual pursuit of happiness properly aligned with the common good. Joe recognizes that we are in a fight for the very soul of America—where we are united despite our differences in facing our challenges—and therefore his policy ideas are principled compromises without compromising one's principles. He eschews party or politics as ever being above the nation, recognizing that it is to the people leaders owe their first allegiance. It is the exact approach that our countrymen and women are demanding from today's leaders, and his book shows the way."

—Joe Sestak, Rear Admiral, USN (Ret.) and former
U.S. Congressman from Pennsylvania

"At a time when progressive and other reasonable Americans are desperately searching for ways to regain the upper hand in the face of the insanity of Donald Trump, Joe Heoffel offers a smart, sensible, and insightful roadmap for us to seize the initiative and lead towards the future. Joe's experience in various levels of government shines through brightly. He's been there, he's done that, and he knows what it will take for us to do it again. You want to know how to appeal to a broader swath of voters? Read Joe's book. It's a great, fun read. And I truly believe we will look back on *Fighting for the Progressive Center in the Age of Trump* as one of the seminal books of our troubled times."

—Daylin Leach, Pennsylvania State Senator, President
of Americans for Democratic Action

"How to fix America's broken politics? This savvy guide from a progressive centrist, featuring socially liberal and fiscally responsible policies, points the way. It's doable, people."

—Carla Seaquist, *HuffPost*

Fighting for the Progressive Center in the Age of Trump

Joseph M. Hoeffel

An Imprint of ABC-CLIO, LLC
Santa Barbara, California • Denver, Colorado

Library of Congress Cataloging-in-Publication Data

Names: Hoeffel, Joseph M., 1950– author.
Title: Fighting for the progressive center in the age of Trump / Joseph M. Hoeffel.
Description: Santa Barbara, California : Praeger, 2017. | Includes bibliographical
    references and index.
Identifiers: LCCN 2017018030 (print) | LCCN 2017030904 (ebook) |
    ISBN 9781440859557 (ebook) | ISBN 9781440859540 (alk.paper)
Subjects: LCSH: Hoeffel, Joseph M., 1950—Political and social views. | United States—
    Politics and government—21st century. | Legislators—United States—Biography. |
    Trump, Donald, 1946—Adversaries. | Democratic Party (U.S.)—Biography. |
    Progressivism (United States politics)
Classification: LCC E901.1.H64 (ebook) | LCC E901.1.H64 A3 2017 (print) |
    DDC 328.73/092 [B]—dc23
LC record available at https://lccn.loc.gov/2017018030

ISBN: 978-1-4408-5954-0
EISBN: 978-1-4408-5955-7

21 20 19 18 17   1 2 3 4 5

This book is also available as an eBook.

Praeger
An Imprint of ABC-CLIO, LLC

ABC-CLIO, LLC
130 Cremona Drive, P.O. Box 1911
Santa Barbara, California 93116-1911
www.abc-clio.com

This book is printed on acid-free paper ∞

Manufactured in the United States of America

To Elsa, Mavis, Luisa, and Nellie

Contents

Preface

On a blustery day in March 1974, in my first campaign for public office, I knocked on the door of a house in Rockledge, Pennsylvania. I was running for state representative as a liberal, idealistic 23-year-old Democrat against an entrenched Republican incumbent in the suburbs of Philadelphia.

A kindly looking old lady came to the living room window, peered out at me around the drapes and shook her head negatively to indicate she didn't want to open the front door to talk. I smiled at her encouragingly, waved my campaign brochure in front of the window, and indicated with hand gestures that she should open the front door. After all, I was her friendly neighborhood politician, and I was there to help.

She responded by producing a butcher knife from behind her back, waving it menacingly in the window, then tapping the knife point on the glass and indicating that it was time for me to get off her front steps and back on the sidewalk.

I complied and my political career was launched. I have enjoyed my time in politics and government. It is a privilege to have a voice and a vote in the public issues of the day. Government service is rewarding and political competition is exhilarating. It is immensely satisfying to help craft a solution to a public policy challenge, or to help a constituent cut some red tape and solve a problem with their government.

Sometimes public life can be a lot of fun. One of the benefits of serving in Congress is the opportunity to impress your family. I tried to wow my wife Francesca while I was on a flight on Air Force One with President Clinton from Washington, D.C. to Philadelphia in 2000 for a bill signing ceremony at Independence National Historical Park. I was duly impressed myself to be on that flight, and as we took off I was eyeing the phone in the armrest of my seat in the VIP section of the plane. The steward had said the phone was at my disposal and all I had to do was pick it up to speak to a communications specialist in the front of the plane who would connect me to any phone anywhere in the world. I stared at the phone for a minute, summoned my nerve, and plucked the phone out of its cradle. The specialist was instantly on the line and I asked whether it was possible for him to connect me with my wife at her workplace. He said he had been waiting for me to pick up the phone, since everybody on their first flight on Air Force One asked to be connected to their spouse, and of course he could connect me. The call went through, Francesca laughed at me, and I sat back and enjoyed the flight.

Sometimes, public life can be embarrassing. Early in my career, I was speaking at an Eagle Scout ceremony at Abington Presbyterian Church in the heart of my legislative district. I spotted an old friend in the audience, a former Eagle Scout himself who was there to help honor the current scouts. I had lost touch with my old friend and had not seen him since we were about 12. Thinking I was funny, I tried to connect with the audience by cracking jokes about how my friend and I used to throw snowballs at cars, which was true, and how the local police used to chase us around the neighborhood, which wasn't true. The audience shifted in their seats and looked uncomfortable. Later over refreshments, I asked a neighbor about the odd reaction from the crowd. He looked at me sharply and asked whether I knew that my old friend had just been released from prison. I was stunned. I wished I had known before I opened my big mouth.

Sometimes, public life can be inspiring. In my first term in Congress in 2000, I traveled to Selma, Alabama, with a number of congressional colleagues to take part in the 35th anniversary celebration of the 1965 voting rights march from Selma to Montgomery. The bipartisan pilgrimage was sponsored by the Faith & Politics Institute and was led by two great men, Congressmen Amo Houghton (R-NY) and John Lewis (D-GA). We met icons of the civil rights movement, toured historic sites, listened to a terrific speech by President Bill Clinton, and walked across the Edmund Pettus Bridge where state troopers had beaten the voting rights marchers 35 years before. The entire weekend was inspiring, but the best moment for me occurred on the first day on the bus ride in from the airport. A documentary film of the historic march was playing on the overhead monitors of the bus, while my colleague John Lewis was slowly making his way down the aisle, quietly talking with members of Congress and answering their questions. On the TV monitors, a 23-year-old John Lewis in a tie and white raincoat was leading the peaceful voting rights march, and then he and the others were being overrun and beaten by the Alabama troopers, while down the aisle 35 years later came the middle-aged John Lewis, chatting amiably with his colleagues. I kept looking at the monitors and the images of John being beaten, and then back at John coming down the aisle toward me. This quiet man's enormous strength gave me goose bumps.

Whether fun, embarrassing, or inspiring, I have worked at my political calling for a long time. As congressman, state representative, and county commissioner, and a candidate for senator and governor, I have 15 general elections under my belt.

The victories have been sweet, the defeats not so much. In the small hours of the night of my first victory in 1976, I found myself suddenly out of bed, dancing around in my pajamas, bobbing and weaving, throwing a flurry of jabs and uppercuts, shadowboxing in the moonlight, and beating the hell out of the world.

The night of my last campaign, a fourth place finish in a four-way primary for governor in 2010, was a lot more subdued. I didn't do any shadowboxing around the bedroom that evening.

So life in politics can be exciting and rewarding, as well as frustrating and deeply disappointing. But in the midst of the pomp and the perks, the joys and the sorrows, the victories and the defeats, there is always important work to get done for the American people. The personal ambitions of elected officials must yield to doing what is right for the greatest number of people. The public good must come before private agendas.

But that is not happening in America today. My frustrations have grown in recent years as I have watched the rich get richer, the poor get poorer, and the middle class get stuck paying all the bills. Income inequality is growing greater year by year, standards of living are not rising as they once did, and economic stagnation stifles hope. People are not as optimistic about the future as they used to be. The American Dream no longer seems to be within everyone's reach.

The country has been put through the wringer during my lifetime. Our failed intervention in Vietnam led most Americans to question the limits of our military power and doubt our abilities to influence events around the world. The lies and lawbreaking of Watergate taught many of us to distrust our government. The false pretenses that led to war in Iraq took a toll on this country and further shook people's confidence in their government.

I remember being convinced that the Nixon administration was lying to me in 1972 when I was a college student. So I marched in protest of the Vietnam War and proudly co-chaired Boston University Students for McGovern. I felt totally alienated from my national government and didn't trust anyone over 30.

By the spring of 2003, when I was serving my third term in the U.S. Congress, I concluded that my federal government was lying to me again, this time about the war in Iraq. I realized I had come full circle. Once again I found that I totally distrusted my national government, but now I was part of that government.

Now, in the Age of Trump, I am more astonished and distrustful than ever before. It is hard for me to tell when Donald Trump is telling the truth, greatly exaggerating, or simply lying. I cannot trust my president, which is a sorry state of affairs for any citizen.

Donald Trump took advantage of our desire for political change and our fears about the economy and won an improbable victory as our new president. But his actions and statements continue to divide the country and raise doubts about the future of our democracy. People either love him or hate him, while he makes no effort to unify the warring sides. The chasm in our body politic grows.

Our national government seems unable to bring people together as our politicians bicker, try to settle old scores, and prepare for their next election.

When I was a young state legislator in Harrisburg we had plenty of partisan battles by day in the state capitol, but we were able to set aside our differences at night over drinks and dinner in the local restaurants. We listened to each other and respected each other. That is missing from today's politics, and we need to get it back.

We can do better. We face three great national challenges: restoring our economic strength, getting our fiscal house in order, and keeping the country safe. We need a plan and a commitment to do all three.

This book promotes the fight for the progressive center based upon my perspectives, ideas, and experiences of 40 years in public life. I certainly do not have all of the answers to the challenges we face. But the lessons of my career teach me that constant obstruction in our government and endless demonization in our politics are not in the public interest. We need to seek common ground to take public action for the public good.

Progressives need to fight for the political center of our civic arena with policies that are both socially liberal and fiscally responsible if we are going to win the battle for public support against Donald Trump.

We need to fight for the progressive center. The time has come to march and protest, to tweet and shout, to make our voices heard, to seek change and reform in the public arena. The fight starts now.

Introduction

The 2016 presidential election demonstrated that national Democrats have lost touch with their working-class roots. The surprising result of that astonishing lapse was the defeat of Hillary Clinton by Donald Trump in an election nearly everyone expected Clinton to win.

Of course, Hillary Clinton actually won the popular vote by a margin of almost 3 million and received 48 percent of the vote to Donald Trump's 46 percent. But the Electoral College, although antiquated, undemocratic, and unnecessary, nevertheless delivered the presidential victory to Trump, fair and square under the rules.

Hillary Clinton did not lose because the Russians meddled in the election, or because John Podesta's e-mails were stolen and disclosed, or because FBI Director Comey violated procedures by publicly discussing his investigation of Clinton's e-mails. Those things happened and they were outrageous. Clinton lost because too many working-class voters did not believe she could change their daily lives for the better.

The hard truth for Democrats is their national ticket underperformed in rust-belt states such as Pennsylvania, Ohio, Wisconsin, and Minnesota where working-class voters hold the key to Electoral College majorities. Clinton's failure to win the expected support in those states from working Americans cost her the election.

Democrats should have known before election night that their political success depends upon fighting for working-class Americans and those struggling to join the working class. It is not sufficient for the Democrats just to rally those liberals and progressives who are willing to use the power of government to help the working class. Democrats must actually talk to those working-class voters and motivate them to come to the polls.

The national Democratic campaign attempted to assemble a winning coalition by appealing to different groups in the party's base with targeted messages, but it was not enough. Democrats failed to deliver a compelling and positive economic message to American workers who are still struggling mightily with the negative effects of the 2008 Great Recession, globalization, and unfair trade.

American politics has not worked well in recent years. During the presidencies of George W. Bush and Barack Obama, excessive partisan warfare dominated the nation's capital, and legislative gridlock usually prevented meaningful action to help the people. Politicians in both parties proved by their actions they would rather fight than compromise. Public action was rarely taken for the public good, and the American people lost trust in their political leaders. The voters became angry and frustrated, and they wanted change.

Donald Trump represents that change. He campaigned for president as a vulgarian. He insulted people and groups left and right and broke many of the rules in the politicians' handbook. He bragged about groping women, mocked a disabled reporter, suggested a religious test for legal immigration, and belittled the parents of an American soldier who died in Iraq. He campaigned as a demagogue who gave the impression that he often does not say what he means or mean what he says.

However, many of those angry and frustrated voters did not seem to mind the many nasty insults and fact-free boasts of the Trump campaign. The voters took Trump seriously but not literally. They were more interested in supporting a candidate who promised to create political change and overcome economic stagnation. The public concluded that Trump could deliver on both counts, and Clinton could not.

Donald Trump's election was a remarkable political success for the ultimate outsider and was the biggest presidential upset since Truman defeated Dewey. Trump's campaign resonated with millions of Americans who quite rightly believe that their government has failed them. But the election also stoked the fears and hatreds of many Americans and left the country deeply divided.

Now, Donald Trump is president of the United States and the Republican Party enjoys solid majorities in the House of Representatives and the Senate. Now in charge, the Trump administration and the Republican Congress are in debt to right-wing conservatives, Tea Partiers, and the white nationalists of the Alt-Right. Team Trump has the votes to enact into the law the most cherished conservative goals of the last decade, including repeal of Obama's Affordable Care Act, reductions in civil rights for religious and ethnic minorities, weakened environmental laws and rules, expanded tax breaks for the wealthy, and promotion of corporate interests at the expense of the best interests of working men and women.

President Trump has a thin skin, a bullying manner, and an oversized ego. He is a fear monger, trying to alarm the public while claiming that only he can save us. He promotes authoritarian policies that are pro-business, anti-labor, anti-environment, anti-immigrant, and isolationist. Many Americans feel excluded from his vision. He will continue to do things in ways no president has done those things before, and his struggles will continue with the partisans and traditionalists in both parties in Congress.

The president seems to relish making corrosive commentaries on social media about critics, opponents, and the mainstream media. The simplicities of his tweets do not match the complexities of governing. President Trump faces a growing credibility gap as the bold actions and glib solutions promised in his tweets seldom occur amid the complicated realities of running the national government.

President Trump and his administration are being investigated by Congress and the Department of Justice for possible collusion with Russian meddling in the 2016 election. As a result of Trump's firing of FBI Director James Comey, another line of inquiry started whether the president obstructed justice by trying to derail the Russia investigation. The Justice Department appointed former FBI director Robert Mueller as special counsel to lead its investigation.

Congress should be interested in public disclosure of all the facts, and the Justice Department will decide whether to prosecute criminal behavior. The country learned after Watergate that the cover-up is usually worse than the crime. In the looming public, legal, and constitutional showdown between the president on one hand and Congress and the Justice Department on the other, Donald Trump will be the big loser.

What is next for our democracy in the uncertain Age of Trump after the unproductive political battling of the Obama and Bush years? How do we escape the clutches of the partisan warriors in both parties and the unpredictable pronouncements and actions of President Trump? Can we find a common ground to achieve good things for the American people?

I believe the answer is found in the progressive center of American politics. We must fight to attain that progressive center by rejecting the partisan extremes and embracing reasonable and progressive policies that will benefit all Americans.

The progressive center is where people of goodwill should come together to reject rigid ideology and embrace fair agreement on public action for the public good. The progressive center is the place for people who believe in a robust public sector, with policies that are socially liberal and fiscally responsible.

The progressive center offers the best opportunity to improve the quality of our lives and to build a secure future for our families. Liberals and moderates and even some conservatives from both political parties should be able to rally together, without abandoning their principles, to provide the leadership and the reform that is necessary to move the country forward.

Progressives understand that government has a valuable and important role to play in our society. Our competitive, profit-driven, free-market system creates boundless opportunities for all and rightfully is the envy of the world. Still, there is an obvious need for a strong safety net provided by the public sector to catch those who cannot compete successfully. There is also an important role for government to play in areas where the private sector falls short: in education, health-care coverage, environmental protection, and old age security. *Progressives* regardless of party embrace the essential role of government instead of demonizing it and work to reform programs that do not work and to implement solutions that do.

The *center* is a vibrant political middle ground where meaningful government action can blossom when public citizens of goodwill seek balanced agreement. The *center* is a broad space of consensus that rejects the apostles of absolutism from both extremes of America's political parties. The *center* embraces policies that are thoughtful, inclusive and, if possible, bipartisan in order to achieve lasting and productive reform.

In contrast, the political right wing promotes policies that are shortsighted and selfish, primarily advocating the interests of the already well off and the well connected. The right-wingers in Congress and the Trump White House want to cut taxes for the wealthy and corporations, while reducing spending for the poor and gutting middle-class entitlements. The Alt-Right movement has brought an ugly white nationalism to the fore of our national politics, and the destructive rage of the Tea Party lingers on in the highest Republican councils. These bitter and angry policies will not benefit most Americans.

Across the aisle, many Democrats still seethe at the obstructionism and invective hurled at Barack Obama for eight years by the Republican Party, and they are outraged that Donald Trump won the presidency although 54 percent of the voters cast their ballots against him. Democrats nurse their grievances and plot their revenge.

The hard-line advocates in both major political parties who clamor for ideological purity, and who want to destroy the careers and even the personal lives of their political opponents, simply do not offer us a sensible way forward. They are not capable of reaching the reasonable compromise that is necessary to make our democratic system work well for all Americans. These partisan warriors threaten our nation's future, both home and abroad. They are dragging down our politics, dividing our government and holding back our country.

America's leadership in the world, and our status as the world's only superpower, is challenged by this endless partisan combat. There was a time during and after World War II when our national leaders prized bipartisanship in foreign affairs and boasted that politics ended "at the water's edge." They quite properly understood that a bipartisan foreign policy is essential in order to present a united face to a dangerous world.

But now, there is a growing and dangerous isolationism in the land, ranging from the "America First" policies of President Trump to the nativist fearmongering of many right-wing leaders. Enflamed by their excessive partisanship, these obstructionists were not able to accept Barack Obama's foreign policy leadership on behalf of the country. Now, they are not capable of working across the aisle to achieve the bipartisan approach necessary for successful American foreign policy.

The question is how do we rid ourselves of the endless partisan warfare and political obstruction that poisons our domestic politics and hampers our international relations.

The answer is to fight for the progressive center in our national politics, while rejecting the partisan calls to battle that come from extremists in both parties. This is how we implement progressive values in a tolerant, rational government that is responsive to all Americans.

We need to ask more of ourselves, while we demand much more from our politicians. We must stop rewarding with our support and our votes the politicians who pander to the extremes in both parties. So many of our elected officials have fallen into a bottomless pit of partisan accusation and recrimination, and the voters too often rally favorably behind those promoting the loudest and most extreme views.

In many gerrymandered congressional districts, where the lines have been drawn to virtually guarantee the victory of the candidate of the majority political party, the incumbents believe they only need to pay attention to the partisan extremes of their political base in order to get reelected. In fact, politicians willing to compromise and do the people's business on a bipartisan basis are often punished, not rewarded, by voters in their next party primary.

We are teaching our representatives the wrong lesson. Our angry and hyperpartisan voting habits lead them to believe it is politically safer to relentlessly fight with the opposing party than to seek meaningful compromise that may be controversial.

We should reward those politicians who, regardless of their ideology, are willing to work together to reach consensus. We must demand that our political leaders stop the mindless obstruction, search across the partisan divide for common ground, and start getting things done for the American people.

We progressives are the ones that believe that government can actually work to help people. We consider government at all levels to be a necessary and positive force that, when properly run, will improve the quality of life for everyone.

So we better make sure that government works effectively and efficiently in America at the end of the second decade of the 21st century. We better figure out how to make government deliver more services in ways that are better, faster, and cheaper. We need to deliver smarter government that provides more opportunities, more common sense, and balanced budgets.

The public wants government to work, with a minimum of waste and partisan bickering and without corruption. Voters want to be led by politicians who have the courage of their convictions, and yet can work effectively with other politicians with different convictions.

What we need to do is to fight for the progressive center in American politics with policies that are socially liberal and fiscally responsible. Then, we must hold that center against all comers from the political extremes and against all ideologues from the political fringes.

Real and lasting achievement in the public arena requires both spirited advocacy of strongly held beliefs and a good faith search for consensus. It is time for the citizenry to demand such achievement, and time for our politicians to stand and deliver.

Here are eight strategies to achieve this success:

1. We must fight to invest in people, while balancing the budget. We must counter the mindless mantra of "starving the beast," which simply cuts taxes and shrinks government. Presidents Reagan and both Bushes supported tax cuts but also increased spending, with the obvious and harmful result of huge deficits. George W. Bush even went to war twice, while cutting taxes at the same time—no president has ever before followed that disastrous fiscal policy. Bill Clinton showed us how to balance budgets with modest tax increases and prudent spending cuts, and Barack Obama tried to do the same in the face of unrelenting partisan opposition. Donald Trump will bring back huge deficits with deep tax cuts for the wealthy and large spending increases on defense and infrastructure. Let's achieve the budget balance we need: everybody pays a little and everybody sacrifices a little so everybody benefits a lot.

2. President Trump's policies of "America First" in foreign affairs, immigration, and trade will overturn decades of bipartisan national agreement on the wisdom of mutual defense agreements, democratic alliances, and

open commerce between countries. We must bolster alliances with Western Europe to deter Russian expansionism. We must fight back against bigoted immigration policies that are untrue to our open and tolerant traditions. If President Trump creates a registry for Muslims in America, then we all must register as Muslims. We must demand fair as well as free trade agreements that focus not only on profits but also on labor, environmental, and human rights standards. Such agreements will level the playing field and allow the American worker to compete more successfully.

3. It is time to balance our budget. Real budget reform requires real political leadership, and two fiscal commissions have shown us how to do it. Deficits must be reduced, revenues increased and stabilized, and the federal budget fairly balanced by following progressive guidelines: achieve a 50–50 split in deficit reduction between spending cuts and revenue increases, share the financial sacrifice among all players and all income levels, focus tax increases on higher incomes, while protecting the lowest incomes from harmful spending cuts, and restore the pay-as-you-go budget rules that helped achieve three Clinton-era balanced budgets.

4. Progressives must stand our ground—defending our principles and values and fighting back against relentless right-wing demonization. We are strong on national security and value bipartisan foreign policy. We are people of faith who must uphold religious tolerance in the face of divisiveness and posturing. We must grow the economic pie for working families and also for the least, the last, and the lost among us. Progressives must take a clear stand on hot button social issues, trusting women to make their own reproductive decisions, supporting gun safety proposals, and defending gay rights and marriage equality. That doesn't mean progressives will make you have an abortion, take your gun, or turn you gay. But we will fight hard on these fundamental issues, and the public must know where we stand.

5. We need more health-care reform, not less, that establishes Medicare for All. Right-wingers demonized President Obama's Affordable Care Act and are now foolishly demolishing it. But Obamacare worked by extending better and more affordable health-care coverage to 20 million Americans and ending unpopular insurance abuses like caps on lifetime coverage and refusing coverage to those already ill. Single payer health insurance is the answer, where everyone is covered and everyone pays, medical providers are held responsible for the quality of their care and the value of their services and are promptly paid, no discrimination in coverage is permitted, financial waste is minimized by simplified administration and universal budgeting, and public health is emphasized through prevention and strong primary care.

6. Politics is broken, so let's fix it. The constant demands of campaign fund-raising challenge the integrity of politics and government. We must eliminate the abuses of gerrymandering and champion three reforms: more government transparency, no more no-bid contracts, and expanded public financing of elections.

7. We need big plans for our big country to restore economic strength and create jobs and to improve public schools and build stronger communities. Let's use public money for public schools, not for private school vouchers, with higher standards, more accountability, and expanded early childhood programs. Let's invest in new jobs and job training, alternative energy and green jobs, and improved infrastructure. Let's spend smarter and grow our neighborhoods by coordinating spending on transportation, economic development, open space preservation, and community revitalization.

8. Bill Clinton showed us how to "bring it" in order to connect with people, and progressives need to bring it every day. We need a farm team that knows how to connect with people in every way: from shaking hands to mastering media relations to using the five basics of making a good and persuasive speech. We need to understand the importance of looking voters in the eye and fighting for things that are meaningful to them, their families, and their futures. We need to stay in touch with our working-class roots if we want to win national elections in the years ahead.

Government frequently fails and disappoints. It was Winston Churchill who pointed out, "Indeed it has been said that democracy is the worst form of government except for all those other forms that have been tried from time to time."[1]

But make no mistake, our current American democracy is not meeting our needs. The election of Donald Trump may be due to angry voters wanting change and relief from economic stagnation, but the Age of Trump is not offering meaningful and rational solutions to our problems.

We can do better. We can take an honest, clear-eyed look at the challenges we face in the public arena, determine what is working and what is not, and then fight for reform and improvement. We can reject the partisan extremes in both political parties and demand consensus and action.

We must fight for the progressive center and make government work well for all of us, leveling the playing field, creating opportunities and improving the quality of life for all Americans.

CHAPTER ONE

Invest in People

On a hot August day in 2004, when I was running for the U.S. Senate, a young man burst out of the front door onto the porch of his family's home in Johnstown, Pennsylvania. He surveyed the scene before him, which included all the noise and commotion it was possible for a Senate candidate and 20 staffers and volunteers to create as we walked out of town. We were trying our level best to attract as much attention as we possibly could. Volunteers were eagerly leafleting both sides of the street, thrusting campaign literature into the startled hands of passersby and homeowners tending to their front yards. The campaign bus—a big RV plastic-wrapped with campaign slogans and eight-foot-high smiling photos of me—was inching up the street, blaring patriotic tunes and rock music through the loudspeakers. I was dashing from one side of the street to the other, dodging traffic and shaking hands. It was a big production.

He took all this in with a steady gaze, this sturdy, towheaded five-year-old boy, then marched to the edge of the front porch, put his hands on his hips and bellowed, "What the hell is going on here?"

That happened well over a decade ago, and I still haven't given that young man an answer to his question. At the time, I couldn't because I was laughing too hard. But he does deserve an answer to his expression of outrage.

In the last few years, there have been a lot of outrages in American public life:

- The depressing presidential general election of 2016. The campaign had no inspiring moments or uplifting themes. Both candidates were unpopular with a majority of Americans. Hillary Clinton is an admirable woman. She had a successful career as a U.S. senator and secretary of state, and she would have made an excellent president. But she was weighed down disastrously by negative baggage partly of her own doing and partly the result of relentless right-wing demonization. Donald Trump capitalized on the anger of working-class Americans with blustery, mean-spirited, and policy-free rants about how he, and he alone, could make America great again.

- The hollow and sterile nature of recent political campaigns by both parties that stress personal foibles and private failings rather than public policy disputes and political differences. The voters cannot learn anything positive from campaigns anymore, and they are fed up and turned off. Only 42 percent of the voting age population voted in the 2014 mid-term elections, which was 7 percentage points lower than 1978, when the U.S. Census Bureau first began asking Americans about their voting habits.[1] Clearly, the voters are uninspired by the tone and substance of congressional campaigns.

- The hyperpartisanship of Republicans in Congress that led to blind opposition to the proposals of President Barack Obama and encouraged strange obsessions and weird theories in the Republican base, and within Donald Trump, about Barack Obama's birthplace, citizenship, and patriotism.

- The corresponding excessive partisanship of congressional Democrats during the Bush and Obama years who let no opportunity pass to blast their Republican colleagues and to highlight their political differences instead of seeking policy agreements. It does not seem to matter which party is in power in Congress. The bickering and obstruction simply goes on and on.

- The curious detachment of President Barack Obama from the nuts and bolts of governing. For example, Obama's Affordable Care Act was truly historic legislation that improved the delivery of affordable health care and added 20 million Americans to the ranks of the insured. But this signature program was weakened by Obama's inexplicable guarantee that everybody could keep their health-care coverage when his plan clearly dictated not everybody could, his astonishing failure to make sure the health-care website was ready for the critically important rollout, and his puzzling unwillingness to defend vigorously the significant benefits of the new law, all of which let his opponents demonize the legislation and convince the public it was bad.

- The reckless lending and greedy self-interested actions of the lords of Wall Street that brought our economy to its knees. Many average Americans lost their jobs, their life savings, and their confidence in their financial security.

- The Cowboy Diplomacy and arrogant foreign policies of President George W. Bush that pushed aside our international friends with unilateral, preemptive strategies that took us to war under false pretenses. Our isolation seemed to make the country less safe, while creating more terrorists than we could kill or bring to justice.

- The human tragedy of Hurricane Katrina and the bungling, incompetent federal response that made matters worse in New Orleans. President Bush's detachment from the scene and grand flyover on Air Force One did not help.

- The feeble congressional enablers in both parties that meekly voted for the Bush tax cuts for the rich, the Bush budgets that hurt the middle class and working families, and the Bush deficit spending which, in the absence of responsible revenue policies, further mortgaged the futures of our children and grandchildren.

William Butler Yeats warned in "The Second Coming" that "the center cannot hold" when "the best lack all conviction, while the worst are full of passionate intensity."[2] Political power resides in the political center in America, even if much of the passionate intensity is on the extremes. We must make the center hold, no matter what outrages occur in public life.

So what the hell is going on here?

We need to start answering that question with a clear-eyed look at the challenges that face us. We need to provide answers that allow us to balance the federal budget and invest in people to improve the quality of life for all. We must reject the right-wing plans to shrink the government and shred the safety net. We must defend our democratic traditions threatened by our new president's authoritarian policies.

The American people have the right to ask that question in the Age of Trump, as economic disparities grow larger between the working classes and the privileged elite, and the order of the day seems to be tax breaks for the wealthy and cozy deals and lax regulation for corporations. The people have a right to ask that question, after years of stagnant wages, soaring health costs, and fewer opportunities for working families. We have every right to ask what the hell is going on, every right to demand that our representatives work together as a matter of course and get some things done for all of us.

The American people value bipartisanship. They want their political leaders to put aside their partisan differences and work together for the good of the country.

The Gallup Poll found on January 19, 2011, that 80 percent of respondents wanted President Obama to work to pass legislation that Democrats and Republicans could agree on, even if it is not what most Democrats wanted, while 83 percent believed it was "extremely" or "very" important that Republican leaders worked with President Obama and Democrats to pass agreeable new legislation.[3] Regrettably, in the years since that poll was taken, partisan gridlock has only become worse and has been the dominant feature of our national government.

As much as the people desire bipartisanship, the party leaders and political bosses hate it. Those politicians thrive on partisan conflict and legislative obstruction that whips up their base, recruits their candidates, pumps up their fund-raising, and motivates their voters. City and county political bosses expect their elected officials to deliver jobs, appointments, and contracts for the party faithful, in exchange for support on Election Day. Bipartisan government, based on shared power and cooperation, while minimizing the influence of party leaders, drives the party bosses crazy.

In 2007, I was elected to my second tour of duty as a Montgomery County Commissioner along with two Republicans, incumbent commissioner Jim Matthews and outgoing district attorney Bruce Castor. The Republicans had always politically controlled my home county in the suburbs of Philadelphia and everyone expected Jim and Bruce to continue that unbroken streak. But the two Republicans did not like or trust each other, and they could not agree on who should serve as chair of the three-member board. That stalemate generated a series of talks and negotiations in the period between the election and swearing-in day, and Jim Matthews and I came to realize that we shared a policy agenda of investing in economic development, transportation improvements, and open space preservation. These commitments would allow county government to create jobs and fight suburban sprawl and traffic congestion. So Jim and I formed a bipartisan coalition to run Montgomery County government from 2008 to 2011 and successfully implemented our agenda on a series of 2–1 votes, while reducing the overall size and controlling the spending of the county government.

Our programs were popular with the public, but the political bosses could not stand it. The two party chairs were ticked off because Jim and I simply would not do what they wanted us to do regarding patronage and appointments. Their highest priority was solid party control, not political reform or good government. The Republican county chair announced a vendetta to drum Jim Matthews out of his party, and the county Republican committee actually voted to censure Jim for having the audacity to share power and form a governing coalition with a Democrat. While my party rank and file liked our partnership, the Democratic county chair did not and ultimately joined the Republican county chair in his public criticisms. They were united in their public opposition to an independent and bipartisan county government that was not run for the benefit or aggrandizement of either political party.

The hyperpartisan behavior in Congress is equally disturbing. The Republicans throughout the Obama presidency opposed every aspect of President Obama's performance, demeanor, record, and agenda. They challenged his domestic program and his international leadership. Their opposition was personal, partisan, relentless, and implacable. In their eyes, Barack Obama was always wrong, and they saw great political advantage in decrying every aspect of his presidency.

The Republicans were encouraged to double down on this confrontational approach by the large majorities they won in the House and Senate in the 2014 elections. Then, the GOP was further rewarded for its partisan roadblocks by its victories in 2016.

It is a great national shame that the voters rewarded, instead of punished, the congressional Republicans for their eight years of political obstruction to Obama.

Congressional Democrats will be tempted to seek revenge and treat President Trump with similar partisan contempt and reflexive legislative gridlock. This would be a big mistake for the Democratic Party. Such excessive partisan opposition surely would accomplish just three things: entertain the extreme parts of the Democratic base, fail to impress anyone else in the country, and accomplish no public good for average Americans.

Clearly, as we proved in Montgomery County, government can work well when political differences are minimized and not allowed to dominate all deliberations. Government can work well when politicians form coalitions and seek consensus in the broad middle ground of American political thought. Government can work well when principled compromise is valued, not scorned, and when the primary goal of elected officials is getting things done, not lambasting each other.

But the right wing in American politics does not agree. They don't like government, they don't like liberals, and they don't like compromise. They want to wage all-out partisan battle until they win total victory. If we are going to move the country to the progressive center, we have to understand our opponents and confront them directly in the public arena.

Starving the Beast

The conservative movement has a simple and understandable two-step program that serves as their foundation and their Holy Grail: cut taxes and shrink government. Cut taxes, mostly for the wealthy, and shrink government, mostly for the poor. And when they do it once, they want to do it a second time, and again and again.

They even have a snappy name for their program. They call it "starving the beast."

Government is the great enemy in the worldview of the conservative ideologues. Government is a beast that needs to be starved into submission. Every problem in America, contend the right-wingers, can be laid at the feet of flabby, corrupt, bloated, and over-spending government.

A conservative celebrity talker, Grover Norquist, famously suggested that his goal was to reduce government to the size "where I can drag it into the bathroom and drown it in the bathtub."[4]

It is snappy, quotable, and simple to understand. Cut taxes and shrink government. Starve the beast.

No question that voters love the notion of tax cuts. They love receiving tax cuts. They are fond of talking about tax cuts. They can even be swayed at election time by promises of tax cuts sometime in the future, no matter how empty or cynical those promises may be.

And who can blame the voters on this score? Everybody would like to pay less to the government in taxes. Nobody readily volunteers to pay more. If taxes must go up, people would just as soon somebody else's taxes be increased, not their own. Senator Russell Long was well known for his adage, "Don't tax you, don't tax me. Tax that fellow behind the tree."[5]

Public officials must be responsive to this anti-tax feeling. They have an absolute duty to watch every public dime, to spend public money prudently, honestly and efficiently, and to cut taxes if that revenue is not necessary to meet the legitimate needs of the people.

So the conservative right-wingers clearly are on to something when they advocate incessantly for tax cuts. They are giving the voters what they want to hear.

But I believe the public is not sold on the second part of the right wing mantra: shrinking the government. The average citizen does not want fewer services, or longer waits for services, or no services at all, from a shrunken government.

People appreciate the government services they receive, and in most cases would like to receive more services. The fact that folks don't like paying taxes, and would love to receive a tax cut, doesn't mean they want to receive reduced government services. And most Americans are very supportive of the long-standing goal of their government at all levels to help those who are less fortunate than they are.

The fact is that service cuts are almost as unpopular as tax increases. Americans want government to offer a helping hand and to maintain a social safety net for the vulnerable among us—they just don't want their tax dollars wasted or stolen. This seems reasonable.

The average citizen understands something that the right-wingers will not acknowledge: in government, you get what you pay for. People want government to provide services, and they know they have to pay for those services. They just want those services cheaper, faster, and better.

People aren't as dumb as the right-wingers think they are. The voters understand that on those occasions when they have voted for advocates of cutting taxes and shrinking government, they have frequently received only some of the former and none of the latter.

The last three conservative Republican presidents before Donald Trump—Ronald Reagan, George H.W. Bush, and George W. Bush—cut taxes, while actually *increasing* federal spending at the same time. This unbalanced and irresponsible fiscal policy predictably resulted in more borrowing, large annual budget deficits, and vastly expanded national debt during their administrations.

These conservative presidents and their congressional supporters actually were feeding, not starving, the beast with borrowed money and more spending. These failed fiscal policies ballooned the national debt and will be paid for by our children and our grandchildren for the rest of their lives.

George W. Bush offers a perfect, painful example of this reckless approach to the federal budget and presidential policymaking. He wanted to starve the beast to cut taxes and shrink government. That is what he campaigned on, that is what his right-wing supporters wanted, and that is what he set out to do. But when circumstances changed, and the real world intervened, he was unable to adjust his political promises when faced with the necessity of governing responsibly.

From the beginning of his presidency in the spring of 2001, President Bush advocated a robust tax cut program that showered the vast majority of its benefits on the wealthy and on corporate America.

I opposed the Bush tax cuts of 2001 as a member of Congress. Even in that pre-9/11 time period, the tax cuts seemed excessive, unfair, and too tilted to those who least needed the help. George Bush had inherited from Bill Clinton a federal budget with a small surplus and was arguing that we should give the extra money back to the people through a tax cut.

Most of my Democratic congressional colleagues and I thought President Bush's tax plan was unfair and was cutting too close to the bone, leaving little fiscal margin for error. We were proud of the Clinton surpluses we had helped to create and didn't want a return to deficit spending. Most of us opposed the 2001 Bush tax plan, but it passed with overwhelming Republican support.

Then came the horror of 9/11.

In the weeks that followed the cowardly terrorist attack on America, Congress and the American people stood behind George Bush, and the president stood tall. His quick response to the fireman who couldn't hear him at Ground Zero—"I can hear you! The rest of the world hears you! And the people—and the people who knocked these buildings down will hear all of us soon"[6]—ranks among the finest extemporaneous presidential remarks in our national history.

Our congressional attempt at inspiring the public was equally sincere but a bit less awesome. The night of 9/11 many members of Congress gathered on the steps of the Capitol in a show of resolve and solidarity called for by our leaders in a late afternoon conference call with the members. After fine speeches by Speaker of the House Dennis Hastert and Senate Majority Leader Tom Daschle, and a moment of silence for the fallen, the assembled members of the House and Senate broke into a spontaneous rendition of "God Bless America." The singing was a bit off key, but the emotion was real, and it was a proud moment to stand there with my colleagues expressing our patriotism.

There was a feeling in the country that everything was changed by the events of 9/11. We were facing a deadly serious challenge from truly evil terrorists, and the continuing work and vigilance of the armed services and the national security agencies took on a new importance and gained a renewed appreciation in the eyes of the public.

President Bush seemed to relish the enhanced attention he received as the commander in chief of a nation that had been attacked and was under a continuing threat. He began to refer to himself as a war president. On a flight on Air Force One in 2002, with four hitchhiking Congressmen aboard, the president was discussing our challenges and policies in Afghanistan when I suggested that we put together an international force of peacekeepers to secure that country. President Bush responded by pounding the conference table and pronouncing, "We are war fighters, not peacekeepers!"[7]

But as President Bush led us into war against the Taliban and Al Qaeda in Afghanistan, he continued to promote and defend his tax cut program. He didn't ask the country for any particular or specific sacrifice to meet this deadly threat to our collective future. George Bush requested large increases in spending on defense and national security, and he received ready congressional approvals since we all recognized the very real threat to the country. But the president continued to support reducing federal revenue through his tax cuts, even while dramatically increasing spending.

If there ever was an American president who could have won overwhelming public understanding and support for limiting tax cuts, or postponing tax cuts, or changing his mind about tax cuts, or even actually raising tax revenue to meet the needs of our national emergency, it was George Bush in the months following 9/11. We would have accepted any sacrifice, financial or otherwise, that the president might have asked of us in the fall of 2001.

But no. President Bush asked for no sacrifice and merely urged us all to go shopping. He continued to promise and implement tax cuts, while increasing spending more and more to defend the country.

The obvious and harmful result was the Clinton budget surpluses were gone in a flash and we were back to deficit spending. The national government was stepping up to keep us safe in the short run, while bankrupting us in the long run.

It is worth noting that never before in our nation's history has a president taken us to war and cut taxes at the same time. Never. It can't be done without a budgetary meltdown. George W. Bush did it twice, in Afghanistan and again in Iraq.

In September 2001, President Bush sought and won authority from Congress to take military action in Afghanistan against the terrorists of 9/11 and all those who supported and harbored them. In October 2002, President Bush sought and won authority from Congress to invade Iraq. These military operations, and all the additional steps taken to improve homeland security and national defense, have cost vast and unbudgeted sums of federal dollars. But George Bush didn't want to ask the American people for more tax revenue to pay for the new spending. He wanted to continue to cut taxes and enjoy whatever political benefit and popularity he believed those cuts brought to him.

So President Bush cut taxes in 2001 and again in 2003 over the objections of progressive Democrats in Congress. We believed that the president's fiscal policy was irresponsible. The predictable and inevitable result was all of the new national security spending was paid for with borrowed dollars that future taxpayers are going to have to pay back, with interest.

The Center for Budget and Policy Priorities reported that the Bush tax cuts would contribute more to U.S. budget deficits by 2019 than the *combined* total costs of the wars in Iraq and Afghanistan, the economic stimulus package, the auto industry bailout, and the revenue lost to the Great Recession.[8]

In short, the center and virtually all other budget experts were predicting a fiscal disaster and budgetary crisis because of inadequate federal revenues and spending beyond our means.

Then came the 2008 election of Barack Obama, which generated excitement and hope throughout the country and around the world. An eloquent and very decent man, his two terms as president strengthened the economy and reduced inflation, the unemployment rate, and the ranks of the uninsured. His presidency improved our relationships and alliances overseas, saved the auto industry, reformed Wall Street, expanded environmental protections, and promoted civil, gay, and voting rights. Barack Obama left our country in better shape than it was following the presidency of George W. Bush.

President Obama quite properly called for Americans to choose hope over cynicism. Nevertheless, many Americans felt let down by the Obama presidency, disappointed that the enduring cynicism in the public arena, which gridlocked our government, swamped the hope for change that Obama originally inspired. His presidency was victimized by the high expectations he created.

President Obama bore some responsibility for the collapse of the "hopey-changey stuff," in Sarah Palin's wicked phrase.[9] He often appeared aloof from the grimy, horse-trading work of lawmaking. He surely cared deeply about enacting progressive legislation, but he appeared uneager to get his hands dirty and never looked comfortable when he tried to pull the levers of power. He embraced the role of our cool, detached professor-in-chief lecturing us about the way forward, unwilling to assume the role of a feisty happy warrior cheerfully battling in the political and legislative trenches.

A quick recap of recent history demonstrates our national frustrations. Presidents Bush and Obama spent trillions of borrowed dollars to bail out Wall Street banks and other financial institutions that had squandered their assets, and also the public's trust, on reckless and greedy lending practices. The bailout of Wall Street worked. The nation's financial system did not collapse as feared, and most of the institutions paid back the federal bailout money. But when people lost their jobs and their savings, they did not *think* the bailout worked. To make matters worse, the banks hoarded their taxpayer-provided funds and failed to make desperately needed loans to small businesses or individuals. Bankers alienated the public even more with fat bonuses for the executives and traders who caused all the problems in the first place.

After the bank bailout, President Obama called upon Congress to invest federal resources to stimulate our recession-wracked national economy by creating jobs and boosting essential spending. So Congress borrowed more money—$814 billion—for the federal economic stimulus package of 2009. The money was spent on individual tax cuts, payments to state governments to boost spending, and investments in public roads, bridges, and infrastructure. Just like the bank and auto industry bailouts, the stimulus also worked. The nonpartisan Congressional Budget Office credited the program with staving off another recession in spring 2010 by achieving modest but essential reductions in unemployment and increases in gross domestic product. But once again, many people did not *think* the stimulus worked, and the country is left with debt that is unsustainably high and must be repaid by future taxpayers.

After the bailouts and the stimulus, majority Democrats in Congress responded to President Obama's progressive budget priorities by passing a federal fiscal plan that restored needed spending to a number of worthy programs starved for support during the Bush era. But Congress failed to meet its responsibility to fully pay for the spending with adequate and sustainable levels of taxation and other revenue, and so both the annual budget deficits and the nation's overall debt grew.

The Republicans in Congress responded to President Obama's proposals by opposing everything he stood for, demonizing both the man and his agenda, and advocating relentlessly for more tax cuts for the wealthy.

To reform the inequities of our health-care system and to cover more Americans with health insurance, President Obama in 2010 passed the Affordable Care Act, or Obamacare, which is the most sweeping social legislation since the passage of Medicare in 1965. Obamacare worked, extending health-care insurance to 20 million Americans and reducing the percentage of uncovered citizens from 20.3 to 13.2 percent.[10] But it was expensive and financed with borrowed dollars, so it added to the federal deficit.

Republican opposition to President Obama's health-care plan and Democratic spending proposals did not lead to thoughtful compromise between the parties on spending and revenue reforms but to increased partisan warfare, which resulted in the government shutdown of October 2013. Following that fiasco, the continuing political rancor made budgetary agreement unattainable, leading to the mindless, across-the-board spending cuts of the sequestration process. These automatic cuts in federal spending certainly helped reduce annual budget deficits but failed to properly meet public needs or thoughtfully prioritize national goals.

Our current budgetary status—born amidst partisan warfare—is comprised of a mishmash of Obama budget proposals, Democratic spending priorities, Republican obstructionism, Bush tax cuts, big tabs for the bank and automobile bailouts as well as for the stimulus package and Obamacare, and the glaring absence of responsible tax and revenue policies. We do not have enough revenue to cover our spending. Our national debt has increased from $10.6 trillion on January 30, 2009, to $19.9 trillion on January 30, 2017, according to the U.S. Treasury.[11] Our national debt is rising sharply every year, and currently stands five times larger than the $4 trillion the federal government spends each year.

Our grandchildren would weep if they understood the burden of debt we are placing upon them.

Economists agree that too much borrowing and unsustainable debt raises interest rates, takes too much money out of the private sector in order to make interest payments, and funnels public resources away from government obligations and programs that desperately need funding.

The fiscal program of President Trump does not seem to include any concern about these negative impacts of our growing national debt. His program includes big tax cuts for corporations and businesses and wealthy individuals. He wants a large increase in defense spending. He wants a massive investment in infrastructure. Trump will simply add to our budget woes.

The impact of Trump spending, taxing, and health care policies will favor the wealthy and really hurt lower-income and older Americans. These policies do not herald a new age of economic populism that will benefit the little guy in our society. This Trump agenda will not help America recover from our painful economic stagnation and income inequality. Progressives must fight this agenda tooth and nail.

Unfortunately, reasonable tax increases remain off the table for most conservatives, even modest measures to ask the wealthy and corporate interests to once again pay their fair share. Instead of budget-balancing tax increases, the right wing wants to cut taxes even further, thus pushing deficits even higher. Their tax proposals would reduce top income tax rates for the wealthy and for corporations. They refuse to acknowledge that reduced revenue makes deficits more likely unless matched with deep and unpopular spending cuts.

So valuable programs are starved and needed spending is curtailed to keep the federal government from going even further into debt. Politicians at all levels of government are unwilling to raise taxes and stabilize revenues due to fear for their own political futures. Essential services to millions of Americans are jeopardized in the process: human services to the most vulnerable, better schools for our children, improved infrastructure for our communities, more economic opportunity, and better health care for many citizens.

Balance the Budget, Invest in People

So, we are back to the old question, what the hell is going on here? The public may sense the shallowness of the right wing two-step mantra of cutting taxes and shrinking government, but conservatives who spout the mantra keep winning elections. Progressives need to do more than gripe about the unbalanced, unfair fiscal policies and cynical proposals of our conservative opponents. We need to advance our own ideas and compete for support in the public arena.

Progressives should offer our own two-step approach to government. At the risk of sounding as simplistic as our friends on the right wing, let's propose that we balance the budget and invest in people.

It may sound too easy, too good to be true. Balance the budget and invest in people. With all of our fiscal challenges and budget problems, can this be done?

In a word, yes. President Bill Clinton actually achieved this two-step progressive program. Clinton balanced the federal budget after years of unbalanced fiscal plans in Washington. Clinton's last three annual budgets actually produced surpluses. He accomplished this with a modest increase in taxes on wealthier Americans and a slight restraint in the growth of social spending. His fiscal plan contributed to, and in turn was greatly benefited by, a booming economy that floated all boats and created 22 million new jobs.

Most Americans remember fondly the strong economy, balanced budgets, and compassionate social policies of the Clinton years. Bill Clinton, with a modest tax increase on the wealthy and some belt-tightening, demonstrated how to balance the budget and invest in people and improve the quality of life in America.

I know from firsthand experience through the years how much Republicans like to criticize Democrats for promoting "tax and spend" policies. Making that charge, accurate or not, really seems to tickle them. And I am the first to agree that there are definite drawbacks to too much taxing and too much spending. But we are worse off with the actual Republican alternative of "borrow and spend."

Instead of cutting taxes and shrinking government, let's balance the budget and invest in people. Let's meet our obligations to help our fellow citizens in need with thoughtful, compassionate, and effective social spending, and keep the country safe with necessary defense spending, while asking all citizens to pay their fair share of the burden and to fully pay for government as we go.

Stop the empty promises and simplistic approach to the voters. Stop the cynical sloganeering and political pandering of tax cut promises, and take the necessary steps to balance spending with revenue. If spending must go up, for whatever reason, then taxes must go up. If spending can be reduced, then taxes can be reduced.

Vice President Dick Cheney famously said, "Reagan proved deficits don't matter."[12] Cheney must have meant that deficits don't matter *politically*, since President Reagan certainly remained popular despite the large growth of federal deficits under his failed version of "starving the beast." But deficits surely matter *governmentally*, since money must be borrowed to cover all the spending, and that money must someday be paid back with interest.

Conventional fiscal doctrine says that during a period of economic downturn, government should not raise taxes or cut spending. The theory

Fighting for the Progressive Center in the Age of Trump

is that any increase in taxes will take money out of the weak economy that is needed to boost private investment and growth, and any cut in government spending will threaten the social safety net needed during a downturn and will reduce the economic pump-priming benefit of public spending just when it is needed the most.

But conventional fiscal doctrine isn't working so well these days. The experts say the Great Recession ended in 2011, but wages remain stagnant and income inequality is greater than ever, even though job growth is up and unemployment is down. Our deficits are unsustainably high and must be brought under control. Our tax policy favors the wealthy and the corporate interests. Our spending is undisciplined and not always focused where it will do the most good for the most people: more jobs, better schools, and stronger communities.

Now President Trump faces many of the same severe constraints that hampered President Obama in promoting economic recovery for all: tight budgets, flat wages, jittery small business leaders, tightfisted bankers, cash-hoarding CEOs, angry voters, and a hyperpartisan Congress. As the Republican majorities and new president grapple with these challenges, the American people are asking with increasing urgency: What the hell is going on here?

The progressive two-step program is the sensible answer. We should balance the budget and invest in people. It will surely take a lot of the first to allow us to do much of the second. But we must do both.

The Balance We Need

Let's balance the budget by generating more tax revenue, while at the same time tightening our governmental belts. Surely the public understands that both higher tax revenues and reduced spending need to be part of the practical political consensus necessary to fairly balance the government's budget. The politicians need to catch up with their constituents in embracing the need for political balance. We need less grandstanding and partisan bickering and more compromise and cooperation.

We need more political balance so we can achieve fiscal balance. There must be more shared sacrifice. It is not fiscally feasible or politically realistic to attempt to balance the federal budget only through spending cuts or only through tax increases.

If the politicians refuse all compromise and insist on a complete budgetary victory for one side and a total defeat for the other, they will inevitably fail and the country will suffer.

We all want to see more politicians with the courage of their convictions. But adamant insistence of the superiority of a conviction can quickly lead to a lack of nuanced understanding and unbalanced action.

In 1983, my wife Francesca and I were traveling through Israel on a trip led by the American Jewish Committee. We visited a settlement in the West Bank that was populated by young Israelis who were committed to expanding Jewish settlements and, in doing so, securing Israel. They believed their collective decision to live in the Palestinian territories was a positive strategy for the safety and future of Israel. They wanted as many Israelis as possible living on all the hilltops near Jerusalem to keep hostile guns off the high ground. We spoke with one young mother who appeared to be in her mid-twenties and already had several children. Our group asked her how many children she planned to have. She answered, "As many as it takes."[13]

That was a woman of conviction. She had the courage of her convictions and was living her life based upon them. We can be inspired by her example but should remain mindful of what happens when the pursuit of conviction is not leavened by a search for compromise and consensus. It is possible, and even advisable, to defend principles while still seeking common ground in the gritty, detailed work of balancing a budget.

So we should strive for fiscal balance comprised of modest tax increases, primarily on higher incomes, coupled with modest spending cuts, protecting services for those with the greatest needs and lowest incomes. Our goal should be that everybody pays a little and everybody sacrifices a little so everybody benefits a lot.

We should abandon the conservative passion for tax cuts for higher income taxpayers and require the wealthy to pay their fair share for the first time since the Clinton era. We should oppose the GOP budget proposals that would simply reduce the top rates for income and corporate taxes.

Instead, we should close the corporate tax loopholes and sweetheart regulatory deals also enacted during the Bush years that favor the few at the expense of so many. This would raise more revenue in a fair and progressive way. Target tax credits to encourage business growth through new investments in plants, equipment, research and development, clean energy, and new job creation. Stabilize government revenues while protecting lower income Americans and working families who already pay their fair share in taxes. Stop wasteful spending, corporate subsidies, dubious congressional earmarks, and unjustified tax breaks for the privileged. Tighten our belts and balance the budget.

Then we must invest in people. Improve public schools and make higher education more accessible. Create jobs through targeted economic development and community revitalization. Strengthen the social safety net and make health care even more affordable. Invest in our people and our communities. Improve the quality of life for all.

How will progressives answer the question of what the hell is going on here? By balancing the budget and investing in people. Clinton did it and Obama tried. Trump is advocating the failed fiscal policies of the right wing. We need faith and resolve for the fight ahead.

That is how we will find and hold the progressive center in American politics, with prudent fiscal policy and compassionate social policy. A government that is socially liberal and fiscally responsible can capture and hold the dynamic center of American politics and govern with assurance and success.

CHAPTER TWO

America First

In February 2001, I traveled on a congressional trip to Russia led by Curt Weldon (R-PA) and Steny Hoyer (D-MD). Curt Weldon had visited Russia many times and had friendships with a number of legislators in the Duma, the Russian parliament, and we were seeking closer relations between our two legislative bodies.

One evening, we had dinner in a restaurant just off Red Square with several Duma members. We were honored by the presence of Viktor Chernomyrdin, who had served as prime minister of Russia from 1992 to 1998. During that time, he formed a close relationship with Vice President Al Gore, and he played a major role in the Russian transition from a planned to a market economy. Toward the end of the evening, after numerous toasts, the large group wanted to pose for pictures. I knelt on one knee in the front row so more people could squeeze into the picture. Suddenly some guy behind me was vigorously rubbing my balding head and shouting in Russian-accented English, "Too much glare! Too much glare!"[1] I jumped up and spun around to confront the wise guy and was immediately enveloped in a Russian bear hug by the perpetrator, who proved to be the great Chernomyrdin himself, roaring with laughter. All I could do was join him.

That easy joshing with Russian leaders seems like it happened in some bygone era. Today, we face a resurgent Russia led by Vladimir Putin who is aggressively determined to restore his homeland to its former position as a world superpower. Putin uses violence at home to silence critics and stifle dissent, and violence abroad to seize Crimea and destabilize Ukraine. He meddles in free elections in America and Europe, trying to undermine democracy and the people's faith in their public institutions. Putin is a bad guy and a threat to international stability. He wants to expand Russia's borders, power, and status. Putin will continue to take military action against neighboring countries if he thinks he can get away with it.

Obviously, it is more important today than at any time since the end of the Cold War for the United States to stand shoulder to shoulder with our allies to make sure that Vladimir Putin completely understands that he cannot get away with it.

But our new president nurtures a strange and disquieting bromance with the Russian leader. Donald Trump seems to believe that his own negotiating skills and the mutual respect he thinks exists between these two tough guys will be enough to overcome Vladimir Putin's passionate nationalism and expansionist goals for Russia. Common sense and knowledge of history indicate that Trump is wrong.

President Trump plays a dangerous game when he scorns our ties to international security agreements such as the North Atlantic Treaty Organization (NATO). NATO has helped keep the peace in Western Europe since World War II and is the best bulwark against the aggressive ambitions of Russia.

The president is correct to demand that our allies pay their fair share of NATO costs and assume more responsibility for their own defense. NATO asks each member country to spend at least 2 percent of that nation's gross domestic product on defense. NATO admits that only five members of the alliance meet or exceed that guideline, with the United States spending the highest percentage (3.6%) in 2016.[2] The other 22 member nations that spend below the guideline must begin to pull their own weight.

But it is also essential that we make clear that a strong NATO is in America's national security interests. It is madness to suggest we may reduce our commitment to the alliance, or even moderate our enthusiasm for our collective defense, for that will only encourage Russia to more aggressively push its expansionist ambitions.

President Trump has proclaimed "America First" as the basis for his foreign, national security, and trade policies. The slogan recalls the misguided isolationist movement before World War II that rendered America slow to react to the threat of Hitler and unprepared for the Japanese attack at Pearl Harbor and for world war.

Since the 1940s, the United States has assumed leadership around the world and embraced open commerce, mutual defense, and democratic alliances as the best way to keep the peace, ensure stability, and create prosperity. In countless acts of enlightened self-interest, we have invested generously around the globe in aid programs, military assistance, and expanded commerce. As a result, America is a beacon of hope, liberty, and freedom around the world. President Trump wants to turn back the clock, withdraw to our own shores, and let the world take care of itself.

"America First" sounds more like "America Only" as presented by the president. This is a selfish and shortsighted policy that will not make America stronger. The United States is the sole superpower in the world and we must stay actively engaged in world affairs. Our leadership in the United Nations, NATO, and other multinational security agreements is vital for our own national security. Our generosity in international humanitarian aid and economic development is both the right thing to do and is in our own best interests.

Free and fair trade remains very important for the economic health and vitality of the United States. Closed borders, high tariffs, and trade wars will hurt all Americans through higher prices and fewer jobs. President Trump promises that his "America First" approach will produce better trade deals for this country, but his negotiating focus needs to be on more than just the financial aspects of trade, the so-called bottom line. Trade with America should involve more than just the almighty dollar.

Our trade deals must also include labor, environmental, and human rights standards. Including such principles in our trade agreements will improve conditions in the economies of our trading partners and will also help to level the playing field and allow American workers to compete on fairer terms with overseas workers.

These reforms will not come cheaply. The cost of imported goods will rise for the American consumer as our trading partners improve their working conditions. The president has promised to bring back manufacturing jobs from overseas, which would also increase prices at home due to higher wage rates and benefit levels for American workers. But these modest costs to the consumer would reap invaluable improvements in our social fabric and community spirit as good jobs return to our embattled working class across the country. Enlightened trade deals that include progressive values are good for America.

Progressives must advocate for our continued robust engagement in world affairs. We oppose the excessive militarism and unilateral policies of George W. Bush and the outmoded isolationism of Donald Trump. We know that successful foreign policy is forged in the bipartisan center of the public square, not on the partisan fringes.

President Trump's "America First" approach to Muslims and immigration has created more problems for America than it has solved. Doubling down on his bigoted campaign promise to ban all Muslim immigration, the new president attempted to temporarily ban all immigration from seven Muslim-majority countries, while asserting that Christians from those countries would receive special admissions treatment. Most Americans, and the federal courts, have firmly rejected any national immigration policy that appears to enforce a religious test on immigration to America.

The president further damaged our national traditions of pluralism and openness by trying to temporarily ban all refugees from anywhere in the world. Our refugee resettlement program does our country proud and offers desperately needed relief and sanctuary to tens of thousands of families threatened in their home countries by politics, unrest, and war. These humanitarian efforts should be increased, not decreased, and should not be used as a scare tactic to drive a wedge between the American people.

President Trump signed an executive order to stop all federal funding, except as related to law enforcement, to cities that have announced themselves as "sanctuaries" from federal immigration policies. The president's order is legally and morally wrong and fails to acknowledge the proper relationship between national and local governments under our system of federalism.

First, the Supreme Court has already ruled that the government cannot withhold federal funding from localities for coercive purposes designed to force jurisdictions to follow unrelated federal mandates. Any withheld federal funding must be connected to the issue the federal government is trying to enforce. So, if Trump wants to punish sanctuary cities for refusing to enforce federal immigration laws, he can lawfully cut off funding only if it is directed specifically at immigrants. Of course, Trump's blanket ban on federal spending improperly goes much further and would effect millions of other urban Americans who receive federal support for a variety of programs dealing with education, housing, nutrition, homeless, and poverty issues.

Second, the Trump ban obviously fails on moral grounds. If Trump has his way, millions of law-abiding American citizens would be denied needed federal support through a number of social programs just because they live in a sanctuary city. President Trump's approach is unfair, hurts many innocent citizens, and is simply wrong.

Third, our system of federalism establishes some areas of government with shared responsibility between federal and local jurisdictions, such as public health and welfare obligations, and some areas with no overlap at all. For example, it is not a federal responsibility to arrest people who run red lights or shoplift from local stores. Nor is it a local responsibility to enforce federal immigration rules. Sanctuary cities are refusing to detain for future federal deportation proceedings those illegal immigrants who are arrested for local violations. In most cases, no federal legal proceedings have started on the individuals, no federal warrants or detainers have been issued, and the police are asked to hold the local offenders for possible deportation simply based on a verbal request by a federal official.

This poses two problems. First, the federal government needs to devote sufficient personnel and resources to carry out its own federal obligations with appropriate legal due process, without trying to involve local government in routine immigration matters. Second, and most important, local police want illegal immigrants to feel free to contact local authorities for protection from unscrupulous landlords, street criminals, or abusive employers without fear that the contact with local police will lead to federal deportation proceedings.

Punishing sanctuary cities by withholding federal funding is truly a bad idea on several levels. But this is not the only bad immigration idea offered by Donald Trump.

President Trump is still insisting on building a wall on the Mexican border that will cost Americans at least $20 billion. After claiming for over a year on the campaign trail that Mexico will pay for the wall, Trump now says that the American taxpayer will pay upfront and Mexico will reimburse us some time later.

Frankly, the government of Mexico will never pay for that wall. Never. Why should they? It is not their wall, not their public works project, not their jobs, not their problem. No self-respecting government would ever succumb to such a financial demand under similar circumstances.

At some point, President Trump will claim that Mexico is "reimbursing" us for the costs of the wall through some future trade deal or economic assistance plan. It will not be true and Mexico will deny it, but Trump will claim victory and just move on. The national debt will be at least $20 billion higher, and the world community will not be impressed.

It is shocking to most Americans that legal entry to our country could be blocked based upon religious beliefs. During the presidential campaign, Donald Trump proposed to ban admission of all Muslims and made a number of threatening comments about imposing surveillance on mosques and creating watch lists and databases for Muslim refugees and even Muslim citizens of the United States. Progressives must fight these religious tests and intolerance with all of our powers.

Peaceful and law-abiding Muslims, who are the vast majority of all Muslims worldwide, are the most effective partners we can have around the globe to fight ISIS and radical Islamic terrorism. Their eyes, ears, and cooperation with their local governments are invaluable as we work with our allies to combat terror and violence against innocent people. The bigoted statements and proposals of Donald Trump about Muslims hurt this country deeply and make us less safe.

I know the first thing we must all do if President Trump tries to establish registries or databases of Muslims in this country, whether for refugees, immigrants, or citizens. We all must register as Muslims. All Americans immediately must go down to city hall or go online and sign up as Muslims through whatever process the federal government establishes. We will proclaim that day we are all Muslims. That is the way for people in the progressive center to trump Trump.

Progressives know that our foreign policy and national security is strengthened when there is bipartisan agreement. In recent years, such bipartisanship in foreign affairs sadly has been lacking.

In the 1930s, there was no more eloquent or rabid opponent of Franklin Roosevelt's liberal New Deal than Senator Arthur Vandenberg, Republican of Michigan. He combined a conservative outlook on domestic issues with a passionate isolationism in foreign policy. He was the stalwart in the U.S. Senate of the traditional Republican principles of balanced budgets and no foreign entanglements.

But all that changed as a result of Pearl Harbor. From 1942 forward, Senator Vandenberg became a supporter of the internationalist foreign policies of Presidents Roosevelt and Truman and provided critical bipartisan support in the Senate. He made a famous Senate speech in January 1945 in which he advocated for U.S. leadership and involvement around the world and endorsed the creation of the United Nations. Events since World War II have demonstrated the wisdom of his policies.

With the phrase "Politics shall stop at the water's edge," Senator Vandenberg popularized the concept of a bipartisan foreign policy that must be united so that America can speak overseas with one voice to friend and foe alike.[3] He will be long remembered as a political leader loyal to his party who set aside his partisan motivations and beliefs because he was more loyal to his country in its hour of need.

Unfortunately, our national leaders are not following the teachings of Senator Vandenberg about the benefits of a bipartisan foreign policy. There continues to be partisan trouble at the water's edge that undermines our national resolve and threatens our security.

Put yourself in the troubled partisan waters that have embroiled our policies in the Middle East in recent years. See if any of this makes sense to you.

Let's say you were a Republican U.S. Senator in 2015. That probably meant that you could not stand Barack Obama and believed that every action he took was unlawful, unconstitutional, and completely wrong. At least, that is how you were acting and what you were saying in public at the time. Let's say you believed your political future hinged on how much you could demonstrate your total opposition to President Obama.

But even under those circumstances, when holding those beliefs, would you have gone so far as to sign a letter to the leaders of Iran designed to undercut President Obama in the middle of his critical negotiations regarding nuclear weapons? Would you have sent such a political message to our menacing adversaries in Tehran, outlining the limits of presidential power and stressing the legislative powers of the president's Senate opponents, which could only weaken the bargaining power and foreign policy of President Obama? Would you have sent such a letter on March 9, 2015, with 46 of your Republican colleagues that was, if not actually treasonous, certainly unpatriotic? If you believe that politics must stop at the water's edge, did this action make any sense at all?

Or, let's say you were President Barack Obama in 2015. You were the commander-in-chief and had been using American military force against Islamic State fighters in Iraq and Syria since August 2014. Iraq had requested you to order air strikes against the terrorists, but Syria had not. Most significantly, Congress had not authorized your use of force. Your unilateral war powers as the commander-in-chief under the U.S. Constitution are limited and are generally understood to be restricted to short-term use of military force to defend the country and respond to attacks. The War Powers Act says you can use force on your own for only 60 days, after which you need the support of Congress.[4] You blew by that deadline months ago. On February 10, 2015, you finally sent a resolution to Congress asking for authorization for the use of American military force specifically against ISIS, limited to three years duration and no ground troops.[5]

But on March 11, 2015, your secretary of state, John Kerry, told the Senate Foreign Relations Committee that you already had the statutory authority to act against ISIS,[6] based upon two outdated congressional war authorizations against Al Qaeda in Afghanistan in 2001 and Saddam Hussein in Iraq in 2002. Why would your secretary of state undercut your request for war authorization by relying on two resolutions that simply did not apply in 2015 to ISIS in Syria and Iraq, based on plain reading of the old resolutions? Why would you allow your administration leaders to suggest that congressional authority for fighting ISIS in 2015 would be symbolically helpful but not required? Why would you not want congressional support on the record for the difficult and drawn-out fight that lies ahead against ISIS?

Or, let's say you were a member of Congress in 2015. The president has asked you, many months after he started using military power against ISIS, to authorize that continued use of American military force. You, not the president, hold the constitutional power to declare war, and you are directed by the War Powers Act to reach a "collective judgment" with the president about the continued use of American military power no later than 60 days after "hostilities" have commenced.

Why weren't you interested in voting on the requested military authorization? Why did you never even consider or debate the president's request? Certainly, there was disagreement within Congress on what limitations, if any, to place on President Obama under the terms of his requested authorization to fight ISIS. There is nothing wrong with a policy disagreement like that, but why couldn't you reach majority agreement on the president's request? Why couldn't you work it out? Why did you not understand the importance of meeting your constitutional and statutory duties to act regarding the exercise of American military power?

If you really held these offices, would you act this way? Of course not, assuming you are reasonable and responsible, you honor your constitutional responsibilities and limitations, and you understand the importance of bipartisan agreement in foreign and military policy. The actual political leaders who acted, or failed to act, as described did so because raw partisan politics has gridlocked our nation's foreign and military policies.

The allocation of war powers between the president and Congress needs to be implemented in a thoughtful and serious way. Important constitutional and political precedents are being set, but the actors are behaving badly.

Every president must honor his or her constitutional and statutory limitations and secure congressional authority, whatever it takes, for continued military action. President Trump needs current congressional authority to continue our world-wide fight against ISIS. Congress should concentrate on granting or amending such military force authorization and stop infringing on executive responsibilities such as negotiating with foreign countries.

Our government's approach to the Middle East is a mess. Politics and partisanship are playing too large a role. The executive and legislative branches need to do their own jobs properly and stop interfering with each other.

The greatest challenge America faces in the Middle East is establishing a just and lasting peace between Israel and the Palestinian Authority. President Trump's announcement that the United States will no longer insist upon a two-state solution to the conflict is a huge setback for our interests in the Middle East and around the world.

No diplomatic achievement would benefit America more than helping to negotiate a two-state solution so Israel and Palestine can exist side by side in peace and security. Such an agreement would improve our relationships with the Muslim world and dispel much of the hatred directed our way. It would bolster our national security, bring peace to a volatile region, protect Israel, and keep faith with democratic principles for all peoples.

Peace between Israel and the Palestinians is the critical step needed to strengthen our standing around the world. Violence and discord are growing in Israel and the West Bank. Palestinian extremists are committing despicable acts of terror against innocent Israeli citizens. The Israeli government is building illegal settlements in the West Bank and the Israeli army is demolishing Palestinian homes. The situation is growing gravely worse.

Throughout the 2016 election, no American presidential candidate highlighted a plan to bring Israel and the Palestinian Authority back to the bargaining table. While the Democratic candidates favored our long-standing and bipartisan commitment to a two-state solution, it was not part of the campaign debate. None of the Republicans during the primaries even mentioned any peace plan on their campaign websites.

President Trump should be advocating for Camp David III—renewed negotiations between the Israelis and Palestinians at the presidential retreat where he personally leads the peace talks.

Many attempts to resolve the Middle East conflict have been tried before. Camp David I in 1978 did bring peace between Israel and Egypt at the urging of President Carter. But at Camp David II in 2000, President Clinton was unable to conclude a final peace agreement between Israel and the Palestinians despite his extraordinary personal efforts. President Obama and Secretary of State John Kerry worked hard for peace in the Middle East in 2013–2014, but to no avail.

America needs Israel and Palestine to exist as two independent and democratic states with secure and recognized borders. The status quo is unacceptable, with frustrations building, violence escalating and hope disappearing. Israel is forced to act as an occupying power to stop violence and protect its Jewish citizens, and that occupation is creating hundreds of thousands of second-class Palestinian citizens whose anger is growing.

Israel must retain its Jewish majority and its democratic status. Palestinians must attain their goals of independence and self-determination.

Borders must be established with mutually agreed land swaps, large and small, that adjust the pre-1967 lines to grant Palestine at least 90 percent of the West Bank. Most of the 500,000 Israeli settlers in the West Bank can be included in an expanded Israel, but the realities of geography dictate that at least 100,000 of those settlers must be physically relocated back to the redrawn Israel with adequate housing provided, or agree to stay and live under Palestinian rule.

The Palestinian "right of return" is a nonstarter. 700,000 Palestinian refugees created by the 1948 Arab-Israeli War, and their descendants now numbering four million, cannot possibly be accepted back in Israel to reclaim their houses and property. But generous compensation must be provided to all refugees.

Jerusalem cannot be awarded in its entirety to one side or the other since the competing claims are too intense. The parties must agree to share Jerusalem with both sides claiming the city as their capital.

Living side by side in peace and security means just that. Palestinians must recognize Israel's right to exist. Both sides must make ironclad security commitments to each other, including promises to punish their own transgressors. Full civil rights must be guaranteed for any minorities remaining in either state. Full cooperation between the parties will be needed to provide both sides with the infrastructure necessary to ensure public health, safety, and welfare.

American leadership is needed more than ever to promote peace in the Middle East. The best way to move forward is for President Trump to commit now to hosting Camp David III and to seek a two-state solution.

Everyone needs to stop the politics at the water's edge. The world is watching, with mouths agape.

Senator Vandenberg had it right, and progressives understand it. Voters are tired of partisan fighting over national security and foreign policy issues. They need to hear the truth, and they need their national leaders to face our national security challenges honestly and without partisan bickering. Let's devise a foreign policy that is bipartisan at the water's edge and allows America to confront our friends and enemies alike with one voice, united and strong.

CHAPTER THREE

Balance the Budget

Josh Shapiró, my chief of staff in Congress, now attorney general of Pennsylvania, rushed into my office one afternoon in the late fall of 2001, shaken and ashen faced, and blurted out that David Obey had taken my earmarks out of his appropriations bill.

This was very bad news indeed for a rank-and-file congressman to have the minority chair of the House Appropriations Committee, Congressman David Obey (D-WI), strip out of the appropriations bill for the Departments of Labor and Health and Human Services the earmarks that I had proposed for related projects in my congressional district.

These spending proposals, which were requested by institutions back home, had received my approval and then were forwarded by my staff to the appropriations committee staff where subsequent review and discussions resulted in their inclusion in the appropriations bill. It was a big and very unwelcome surprise for the Democratic chair of both the Appropriations Committee and the "Labor H" subcommittee to reach back into the bill just before House consideration and strip out my earmarks.

I asked Josh what had gone wrong and he simply didn't know. Josh had been advised by committee staff that the chairman had taken out the agreed-upon earmarks without explanation, and there was nothing further Josh could do at the staff level. He told me I had to speak to Obey.

Congressman David Obey was a fine public servant. He retired from Congress in 2010 after ably representing Wisconsin's Seventh District for over 40 years. A fiercely partisan Democrat renowned for his tenacity and skill in congressional trench warfare, Obey was one of the most liberal members of the House in the outstanding progressive tradition of Wisconsin's legendary Robert La Follette.

But you didn't want to mess around with Dave Obey. He was outspoken and blunt and somebody you wanted on your side and in your foxhole if you had to go to political war. He used to refer to himself as a grumpy old man, and sometimes he fit that bill. But he was highly respected in the Democratic caucus and I had always enjoyed a good relationship with him. So I knew I must have a major problem if Chairman Obey had yanked my earmarks.

I found Dave on the House floor and as soon as I sat down next to him he let me have it with both barrels. He was furious over remarks I had made during congressional debate a few days earlier. During a standard debate colloquy, I had agreed with another Democratic colleague of ours from Florida on a controversial point involving American policy regarding the Israeli-Palestinian dispute. I was unaware that this particular topic was the subject of a huge and bitter dispute between my two colleagues. Obey wrongly concluded that I was actively conspiring to gang up against him. He told me that when he saw our debate on his office television a few days before, he had picked up his phone and instructed his staff to eliminate my earmarks from his bill.

I was stunned but recovered quickly enough to explain the situation, declare my innocence, and apologize for the misunderstanding. David looked at me for a second, smiled and said he now understood the circumstances and he accepted my apology, and we shook hands on it. By the time I got back to my office, a relieved Josh Shapiro greeted me with the welcome news that the appropriations committee staff had just called him to advise that my earmarks were back in the bill.

That was that. Problem solved and we all moved on. Within a few days, the appropriations bill passed the House with my earmarks included.

But as I look back, it is now clear to me that the entire system of budget earmarks was a mess. Members of Congress should not have the power to direct federal spending to particular projects and institutions back home without rigorous legislative and public review. Committee chairs should not have such make or break power over rank-and-file members. We should no longer tolerate budget earmarks and other financial gimmicks at any level of government.

According to Citizens Against Government Waste, spending on federal earmarks peaked in 2006, when members of Congress diverted $29 billion for projects back home. But earmarking was cut back due to public opposition and bad publicity surrounding federal pay-to-play prosecutions based on campaign donations from beneficiaries of earmarks. The 2010 federal budget contained about $16 billion in earmarks, and new appropriations rules in the House banned earmarks to benefit for-profit corporations.[1]

In 2011, Congress enacted a "temporary ban" on the formal system of earmarking money in appropriations bills through a formula based upon seniority. But the budget games continued, and the practice of earmarking never really went away.

In November 2015, Citizens Against Government Waste reported that earmarks still existed but were now included in the 2,000 page Consolidated Appropriations Act of 2016, which contained all discretionary spending for the year. This consolidation simply made earmarks much harder to spot than in prior years when Congress followed usual procedures and approved the federal budget in 12 separate appropriations bills.[2]

Now, as President Trump and Congress grapple over the federal budget for 2018 and beyond, congressional Republicans are talking about lifting the temporary ban on earmarks and formally reinstituting the process, only this time calling it congressionally directed spending.

We need fundamental budgetary reforms throughout government, as well as a commitment to balancing the federal budget in a fair and progressive manner. We must get our national fiscal house in order.

No More Earmarks

Although I eagerly participated in the earmarking process for the six years I served in Congress, I now believe that earmarks created more problems than they were worth and should be eliminated.

Let me note that earmarks were not evil nor were the people who sought them. Organizations and institutions back home have every right to seek federal money for their programs, and members of Congress have every right and even a duty to seek federal appropriations for their districts and states.

Earmarks are so named because the practice allowed individual members of Congress to designate or "earmark" in spending legislation a specific amount of money for a particular project or institution back home. The earmarked money would have been appropriated anyway to the relevant federal agency or department. Earmarks did not increase federal spending, but they did reduce the amount of money that the particular department would receive in general funds to use at its own discretion to meet its regular obligations. Specific earmarks were inserted in one of the 12 annual appropriations bills that are passed by Congress to fund the federal government and required a particular agency to use a specific sum of their general appropriation for an earmarked project.

Defenders of the practice maintained that earmarks allow elected officials, who were closest to the people, to have more control over federal spending than nameless, faceless bureaucrats who would otherwise spend the money, and that argument has some merit.

But in reality, the federal bureaucrats have a job to do and limited resources with which to do it, and they generally make their decisions and carry out their duties objectively and without favor or bias. Politicians, on the other hand, have to respond to the public and win elections and are always tempted to reward donors or favor large employers back home. It is tough for an elected official to be objective about the greater needs of society when there is a pot of federal money available and he has a chance to grab some of it for a project in his district.

There is no question that politics played a role in earmarking, and sometimes the political initiative came from the executive branch. In the summer of 2000, I was running for my first reelection to Congress and Bill Clinton was enjoying his last summer in the White House. My chief of staff Josh Shapiro received a call from a White House staffer asking if I could use a $10 million federal transportation grant for my district in the 2001 budget then under consideration. Josh immediately said yes, and then called me to share the good news and to figure out if there was a worthy project back home that would qualify for this unexpected money. We agreed he should call the Montgomery County, PA Planning Commission in my district and speak to the chief transportation planner, Leo Bagley. Sure enough, the county planners had a long cherished but unfunded concept to extend a little used, dead-end road along the mostly abandoned riverfront in Norristown, the county seat, and to connect the road to a proposed interchange on the Pennsylvania Turnpike a couple of miles away. This project would not only double the road access to and from the county seat but would also open up the neglected riverfront for badly needed economic development and revitalization. Needless to say, Josh and I moved quickly to nail down the funding, and the $10 million was earmarked in the federal budget. This transportation project, now known as the Lafayette Street Extension, is underway and will cost at least $150 million, including the new turnpike interchange. The project will transform Norristown's riverfront and bring growth and opportunity to the county seat. The county might still be looking for the first $10 million if Bill Clinton wasn't looking out for a first-term Democrat in 2000 facing a tough reelection battle.

Earmarks had become such a part of the federal appropriations process that the whole operation was institutionalized and run based upon seniority, committee assignments, and status in the majority or minority party. There was a numerical formula that was used to determine how many dollars each member was entitled to receive in earmarks in the appropriations bills, with senior members and leadership getting the most and junior backbenchers getting the least. I remember in my third and final term in Congress, I was entitled in the upcoming transportation reauthorization bill, based on my status as a first-term member of the Transportation and Infrastructure Committee, in my third term in Congress, and a member of the minority party, to transportation earmarks worth $10 million. Other members were entitled to different amounts, depending on their committee assignments and seniority.

Certainly, an outright ban on earmarks won't end the desire or the ability of savvy legislators to bring home the bacon. Senior members of Congress and committee chairs will have success with "phone-marking" where they can pressure department and agency heads over the telephone to spend parts of their budgets on a project or two in that lawmaker's district. Members of Congress in the president's party have always had success through the years seeking support from the administration for federal spending on projects and priorities back home. Governmental spending decisions will never be fully objective or removed from politics.

As controversial as the federal earmarking process became, it was far better in terms of merit, objectivity, and accountability than the system used in state government in Pennsylvania for many years. In Pennsylvania, the legislature and governor would insert into the state budget specific funding directives called WAMs, or Walking Around Money. WAMs were cherished by the legislative sponsors and community recipients but denounced by open government advocates and budget reformers.

Actually, I believe I was the recipient of one of the very first WAMs in state history. It was the summer of 1977 and the state was in midst of a prolonged budget fight. I was a first-term state legislator and was struggling with my colleagues to pass the overdue state budget that should have become law by June 30. In spite of unpaid state workers, unmailed welfare checks, and other unmet state obligations, the budget impasse dragged on and on. Nobody knew when the logjam would break or when the leadership would bring the budget bill up for a final vote.

As the budget vote was finally approaching in mid-August, I was called to the office of the Democratic Majority Leader, State Representative James Manderino. Big Jim was already legendary as a masterful politician and forceful legislative tactician who ran the Democratic caucus with an iron fist. I was already a "yes" vote for the budget Jim was supporting, so I was a little surprised that he would spend any time with a lowly freshman when he had more votes to round up. But he wanted to reward me for my loyalty and support for the Democratic agenda, and he knew I would have a tough reelection after I voted for the tax increases that the upcoming budget would require.

Jim Manderino took me by surprise when he said I could designate $7,000 in the budget of the state parks department as a grant to any parks and recreation project I wanted. He said the administration of Governor Milton Shapp had agreed to this budget procedure to reward its allies. Big Jim gave me a wink and said that most members supporting the budget were getting $3,500, but since he liked me I was getting a "double" grant. This sounded very good to me, and I quickly designated as the recipient of the grant the Abington Township Department of Parks and Recreation in my hometown, where I knew the unanticipated state funding would be put to good use. This funding coup was well received back home.

From that modest beginning, the tradition of WAMs in Pennsylvania grew into a budgetary monster. State dollars were squirreled away in the budgets of a number of executive departments in five lump sums in each department. By long-standing custom established by both parties, the governor controlled one pot of money in those departments, and the four leaders of the House and Senate party caucuses controlled the other four pots. All that the leaders or the governor had to do was call the secretary of the department and direct that a specific grant of money be sent to a designated local project, courtesy of the local legislator. There was no public notice, staff review, or legislative votes concerning these projects. The practice afforded the legislative leaders tremendous control over their rank-and-file members, since the leadership could grant or deny the WAM requests of their caucus members without any public accountability. Predictably, the leaders used their extraordinary power over WAMs to reward loyal supporters in their caucus and to punish independent or uncooperative legislators.

Supporters of WAMs in Pennsylvania made similar arguments as supporters of federal earmarks—it is better to allow the elected officials rather than the bureaucrats to make these decisions affecting local projects. And there is no question that thousands of very worthy fire companies, libraries, schools, and nonprofits received these WAMs in Pennsylvania and made very good and appropriate use of the state money. But the lack of budgetary review and authorization and the absence of public accountability were shameful, as was the use of WAMs by legislative leaders to keep in line the rank-and-file members of their caucus.

We should replace the discredited system of federal earmarks and state WAMs with a more transparent and accountable process that is still capable of identifying and funding worthy local projects.

The answer is to use the regular appropriations process at all levels of government without the little shortcuts, special handling, and insider favoritism that currently creep into the process. If a local project is worthy of federal or state funding, then it will survive a fair scrutiny by committee staff and can be reviewed as a regular line item in the budget with appropriate openness and public accountability. No need to insert the projects in a conference committee report at the end of the legislative process with little public scrutiny, and no need to create lump sums in executive departments under the private and personal control of legislative leaders. If the projects are not worthy, they should be weeded out during the regular legislative process of committee hearings, amendment votes, and debate and final passage by the full legislative body. It will require a thoughtful and painstaking process, and perhaps an expanded staff, but the result should be more openness, better projects, and improved fiscal discipline.

But a harsh reality remains—even if we totally eliminate all earmarks and WAMs, the budget crisis facing our governments will still be staring us in the face. As progressives, who want government to have both the resources to improve the quality of people's lives and the solid public support to sustain the social safety net and other worthy programs, we have to figure out how to balance budgets, particularly in Washington, D.C., so that we can then invest more in people and create better opportunities in America.

There are a lot of Americans who are skeptical of our track record. Many Americans believe we progressives tax too much, spend too much, and simply care too much about solving everyone's problems by spending other people's money. The 2014 and 2016 election results, which resulted in Republican legislative majorities in Congress and in many states, show that millions of Americans agree with these criticisms.

If we are going to succeed in moving a majority of the American people to the progressive center of our national politics, we have to demonstrate our ability to manage government and its tax revenue efficiently, fairly, honestly, and compassionately. Eliminating federal earmarks and reforming state abuses like Pennsylvania's WAMs is all well and good, but it is absolutely critical for the future of the country, and for the credibility of the progressive movement, for us to get serious about controlling federal deficits, reducing the national debt, and balancing the federal budget.

Getting Our Fiscal House in Order

We have already discussed in Chapter One the fundamental need in America to balance our federal budget so we can invest in our people. We know the current level of borrowing and spending is unsustainable, as is the crushing level of debt caused by all that borrowing and spending.

Granted, extraordinary federal spending was necessary in 2008–2010 through the bank and auto bailouts and the first federal stimulus package to keep our economy from complete collapse, and those programs certainly succeeded in keeping the Great Recession from becoming another Great Depression. Subsequent decisions by President Obama and Congress to continue the Bush tax cuts, to extend unemployment compensation, to reduce the payroll tax by nearly one-third, and to grant other tax relief amounted to a second stimulus plan larger than the first and were designed to spur the economy further and bring recovery sooner. Of course, the increased spending and decreased tax revenue will make our national debt that much larger.

So we know what we have to do. Balance the budget in the long run by generating more tax revenue, while tightening our governmental belts.

The only balanced program that will fairly balance the budget is obvious: modest tax increases, primarily on higher incomes, coupled with modest spending cuts, protecting those with the lowest incomes. Everybody pays, everybody sacrifices, everybody benefits.

It is time for our national leaders to act like leaders. We got ourselves into this budget mess, and we can get ourselves out.

It is certainly time for President Trump and the members of Congress to acknowledge that we cannot responsibly on a long-term basis continue our current fiscal policies. If we want to invest in economic recovery and infrastructure improvements, provide a strong social safety net, keep the country safe from outside threats, and reduce our overwhelming and harmful debt, then we cannot continue to cut taxes across the board for everybody. If we try to do all of these things, we will have a budget meltdown and fiscal disaster.

Two thoughtful deficit reduction plans were presented in the late fall of 2010 to the president, Congress, and the American people. These studies provided a blueprint to the country for the tough, painful, and necessary steps that must be taken to balance our budget and to get our fiscal house in order. It is not necessary to agree with every recommendation of either commission in order to move toward a resolution of these difficult challenges. But it is necessary to agree on the problem, sit down together like adults, and use the commission findings as a guide to reach agreement on solving the problem.

The National Commission on Fiscal Responsibility and Reform issued the report that received the most attention. Commonly referred to as the president's deficit reduction commission, it was cochaired by Senator Alan Simpson, former Republican Senator from Wyoming, and Erskine Bowles, former Democratic chief of staff for President Clinton.[3]

Its fact-finding was candid and clear-eyed, its recommendations equally so. The commission did not pull its punches: "Our nation is on an unsustainable fiscal path, spending rising and revenues falling short, requiring the government to borrow huge sums each year to make up the difference. We face staggering deficits . . . [T]he escalation was driven in large part by two wars and a slew of fiscally irresponsible policies, along with a deep economic downturn. We have arrived at the moment of truth, and neither political party is without blame."[4]

The commission's report goes on, painting a dismal picture. "Even after the economy recovers, federal spending is projected to increase faster than revenues, and so the government will have to continue borrowing money to spend. The Congressional Budget Office (CBO) projects that if we continue on our current course, deficits will remain high throughout the rest of this decade and beyond, and debt will spiral ever higher, reaching 90 percent of GDP in 2020."[5]

The commission prescribed some tough medicine to solve the problem. It set a goal of reducing the debt by $3.8 trillion by 2020 and reducing annual deficits from $1.4 trillion in 2010 to $400 billion by 2015. The commission recommended cutting defense spending, eliminating by one-third the number of overseas bases, freezing military pay, reducing the federal workforce by 10 percent, cutting farm subsidies by $3 billion per year, reducing Social Security, Medicare and Medicaid spending by $733 billion over 10 years, while raising the retirement age gradually to 69 by 2075, cutting discretionary domestic spending by $1.4 trillion over 10 years, reducing tax breaks for higher incomes, increasing the federal gas tax by 15 cents per gallon, raising the income cap on Social Security taxes, and increasing fees for national parks.

This report was a bitter pill to swallow. The second report did not taste any better.

The second deficit reduction report and plan was issued by the Bipartisan Policy Center, founded by former Senate leaders Howard Baker, Tom Daschle, Bob Dole, and George Mitchell. The center appointed a Debt Reduction Task Force, cochaired by Senator Pete V. Domenici, former chairman of the Senate Budget Committee (R-NM), and Dr. Alice M. Rivlin, former director of the Office of Management and Budget, and the first director of the Congressional Budget Office.[6]

The Domenici-Rivlin task force painted a sad picture of where we are and where we are going, similar to the Simpson-Bowles report. The task-force recommendations were equally tough, and the reports were in agreement on numerous points. They both recommended the delay of spending cuts to allow the fragile recovery to take root first. They both would lower income tax rates, while eliminating and modifying most exemptions in order to raise more revenue in a more equitable manner. The task force also suggested a new 6.5 percent national sales tax with exemptions to protect lower income taxpayers, and a one year "payroll tax holiday" to spur spending and create jobs.

The Simpson-Bowles report makes the very valid point that Social Security needs to be reformed and made fiscally sustainable for its own sake, not just for the purposes of deficit reduction.

I agree with the approach of the Domenici-Rivlin report that seeks to balance spending cuts and tax increases on a roughly 50–50 basis. That seems the most equitable way to proceed. It is important for the purposes of reaching consensus not only for everyone to sacrifice to achieve a balanced budget but also for everyone to know that everyone else is sacrificing, too. A clear way to achieve that is for deficit reduction to be shared equally between tax increases and spending cuts. That way, everyone's ox gets gored.

The importance of these two reports is found in the clarity of the alarms they sound and in the candor and wisdom of the recommendations they offer. It is long since time to pay attention and take action.

The *New York Times* published a remarkable piece on our budget challenges on November 14, 2010, that remains relevant today.[7] The editors included what they called "an interactive graphic" designed by reporters David Leonhardt and Bill Marsh to allow readers to ponder a number of budget options for cutting spending and raising tax revenue. The goal of the exercise was for readers to try to cut $1.345 trillion from the federal budget by 2030. This exercise afforded people the opportunity to evaluate the tough budget options facing national policymakers.

In order to give readers lots of options to achieve the target of $1.345 trillion in deficit reduction, the *Times* offered a menu of annual budget choices almost triple the amount of spending cuts and revenue hikes needed to plug the deficit. The graphic contained 23 possible spending cuts totaling $1.81 trillion and 16 potential revenue raisers totaling $1.955 trillion. The cost of each possible spending cut or tax increase was estimated to the nearest $5 billion.

The 23 possible spending cuts ranged from small ticket items like eliminating farm subsidies for a savings of $15 billion, or cutting foreign aid in half (also $15 billion), or reducing the federal workforce by 10 percent (also $15 billion) to some big impacts such as increasing the Medicare eligibility age to 70 from 65 ($105 billion), or raising the Social Security retirement age to 70 ($245 billion) to capping Medicare growth at GDP growth plus 1 percent ($560 billion).

The 16 possible revenue raisers included interesting choices like exempting the first $5 million of an estate and taxing the rest at 35 percent to raise $20 billion (the 2011 Obama-GOP compromise), or exempting only the first $1 million of an estate and taxing the rest at variable rates to raise $105 billion (the former policy under Clinton). Larger tax increases included reducing the mortgage deduction and other tax breaks for high income households to raise $55 billion, or gradually raising the tax on carbon emissions starting at $23 per ton ($70 billion), or gradually reducing the tax break for employer-provided health insurance ($155 billion), or imposing a 5 percent national sales tax, exempting education, charity and housing ($280 billion).

The point of this challenging exercise offered by the *New York Times*, and the significance of the two deficit reduction reports, is that many options exist for national policymakers to bring our annual budget deficits and national debt under control. They can raise revenue through tax increases and reforms and save money through spending cuts. If they are thoughtful, they can achieve this deficit reduction fairly and equitably. But to be thoughtful, they have to start thinking clearly and courageously.

President Obama should have announced his support for one or both of the two deficit reduction reports, even if he had to hold his nose while he did it. He could have indicated his unhappiness with some of the provisions, or called for further refinements, or just have started the conversation, but he essentially ignored both reports. That was a very unfortunate failure of leadership. The president of the United States is the indispensible player in this budget drama and only he has the power to bring the other players together to debate a comprehensive solution.

Now President Trump has the opportunity to accept his fiscal responsibilities, embrace the recommendations of these reports, and lead the country to sound fiscal policies. Bluster, wishful thinking, and alternative facts will not get the job done.

Since the two reports were issued, little long-term progress toward balancing the budget has been accomplished, but a great deal of energy has been expended in fruitlessly debating competing proposals and pointing fingers across the partisan divide.

In 2011, the Republicans in Congress refused to approve an increase in the federal debt ceiling because they wanted to blame President Obama and the Democrats for too much spending, even though the Bush tax cuts of 2001 were at least as responsible as any excessive spending for the increased debt and the need for more borrowing.

The debt ceiling deadlock was finally broken by the passage of the Budget Control Act of 2011 that created the so-called super committee of House and Senate members charged with finding budget savings. If the committee failed, then the law provided that automatic, across-the-board spending cuts, called "sequestration," would occur.

The much-ballyhooed super committee failed spectacularly and could not reach agreement on anything. It was an absolutely pathetic performance. The super partisans on the committee were not willing to give an inch. Accordingly, the sequestration cuts took effect, which did reduce spending but pleased nobody because such cuts reduce all program spending by the same percentage without evaluation of what is working best and what is most important.

Then the country was treated to the hyped debate regarding the approach of the "fiscal cliff" on January 1, 2013. This feared crisis was caused by the pending expiration of the 2001 Bush tax cuts, which had been extended by Congress for two years in 2010, and more sequestration spending cuts. The fiscal cliff would have increased tax revenue by 20 percent and reduced spending less than 1 percent on the first day of the year. That surely would have created the benefit of significantly reducing our annual deficits and national debt, but economists feared that the abrupt changes would lead to further economic recession.

So Congress responded by passing last minute legislation that reduced the tax increases from 20 percent down to 8 percent and allowed spending to increase 1 percent, thus avoiding a shock to our economy.

But little has been accomplished substantively in recent years by all this gnashing of political teeth in Washington, D.C. to actually make difficult and sensible budget decisions on spending and taxation.

The annual legislative process in Congress essentially broke down in the later years of the Obama presidency, and little progress was made in resolving our serious fiscal problems. Because of excessive partisanship, neither the president nor either political party was willing to compromise or seek common ground. Accordingly, Obama and Congress basically put the budget on automatic pilot. Each year, Congress missed the deadlines for passing the 12 annual appropriations bills, and each year at the last minute Congress would pass and President Obama would sign a comprehensive and consolidated budget bill that simply continued the spending priorities and levels from the previous year, along with inadequate tax revenues. No progress was made and tough decisions were delayed.

The 2016 presidential election did not include any real debate or offer any good ideas on how to solve our budget challenges. Now, President

Trump is pursuing his campaign promises to spend more and tax less. This will only make the problem worse.

We are a very long way from putting our fiscal house in order. But achieving a fair, progressive balance of the income and outgo of our government's money is critically important to our economic well-being and civic happiness. We need more presidential leadership and a Congress filled with adults to resolve our budget challenges.

Haven't the Rich Suffered Enough?

A critical requirement of any major shift in tax policy is that we restore a better balance between the tax burden placed on wealthier taxpayers compared to middle- and lower-income wage earners. Unless you subscribe to the belief that the rich have suffered enough, it is hard not to conclude that wealthier Americans have been very well treated by recent tax policies and really need to start paying more of their fair share of federal taxes.

The progressive author and blogger David Sirota posted an insightful column in July 2009[8] pointing out that the wealthiest 1 percent of Americans had the highest share of total national income since 1929 and were paying the lowest tax rates on that income in the last 20 years. The Bush cuts of 2001 and 2003 dropped the tax rate on the highest income level down to 35 percent from the prior Clinton level of 39.5 percent. That cut saved the 1 percenters over $700 billion in taxes, by Sirota's calculation. Fundamental fairness dictates that our national tax policy should ask more of the very wealthiest citizens in the country.

Mark Zandi, chief economist of Moody's Analytics Inc., has identified about $1 trillion of "tax expenditures" in our annual federal budget, which totals about $4 trillion, including tax exclusions, exemptions, deductions, and credits.[9] He believes, and I agree, that these tax expenditures closely resemble actual government spending. Zandi states, "A deduction for local property taxes is no different from the federal government's sending checks to homeowners." Zandi believes that when we cut tax expenditures it is the same as cutting government spending, which we must do to reduce deficits. He argues that most tax expenditures favor higher income taxpayers who itemize their tax returns and thus claim the benefits, and so reducing tax expenditures will help restore fairness to the tax code.

The nonpartisan Campaign to Fix the Debt is promoting an inclusive, broad-based, and bipartisan approach by business, civic, and political leaders to urge our elected representatives in Washington, D.C. to get serious *now* about fixing our long-term debt and deficits.

The campaign is not pushing any one plan in particular but supports the following five core principles:[10]

1. Pass a budget that reduces the debt path and reverses the current trend of debt growing faster than the economy.
2. Focus health-care reform on cost control, make sure health reforms do not add to the debt, and do extend the solvency of Medicare.
3. Enact fiscally responsible tax reform.
4. Pay for all new initiatives by offsetting the costs of all new spending or tax cuts.
5. Seek spending reforms in Medicare and Social Security.

The Campaign to Fix the Debt believes the recommendations of the Simpson-Bowles Commission, the Domenici-Rivlin Task Force, and other recent bipartisan efforts provide a sensible game plan for restoring our fiscal health, promoting long-term economic growth, and protecting the vulnerable.

Guidelines for Fiscal Sanity

I suggest the following eight progressive guidelines as we move forward with the serious effort that is badly needed to reduce budget deficits, shrink the national debt, promote tax fairness, and restore fiscal sanity:

1. Achieve a 50–50 split in deficit reduction efforts between spending cuts and revenue increases. This is the fairest approach that will involve all economic sectors.
2. Mandate some shared sacrifice among all the players and all the income levels. Everyone must suffer some pain and be part of the solution.
3. Focus tax increases on higher incomes and protect the lowest income earners from harmful spending cuts. We should tax based upon ability to pay and protect the social safety net for those most in need.
4. Allow manual laborers, and other occupations with physical wear and tear, to claim Social Security/Medicare benefits at a lower age, while the retirement age generally rises for others.
5. Ask the 1 percenters to pay a fairer share of the tax burden. The rich continue to get richer, so their tax burden should keep up, too.
6. Ask every beneficiary of universal health coverage to pay something to finance the coverage. This will give all a vested interest in health care and will help to control costs. FDR did this for Social Security, and LBJ did the same for Medicare, by using payroll taxes to finance those programs.

7. Use budget restrictions and health-care competition to control spending and improve already high levels of efficiency in Medicare and Medicaid.

8. Restore pay-as-you-go budget rules that helped achieve Clinton-era balanced budgets by requiring any increase in spending to be offset by a comparable decrease in spending or an increase in tax revenue elsewhere in the budget.

It is time to get serious about putting our fiscal house in order. It is time to end the budget abuses and gimmicks and to take real action to reduce budget deficits and to bring our federal budget into balance once again. A progressive president, Bill Clinton, achieved three balanced budgets by the end of his presidency along with a strong and growing economy, and I believe we progressives can do it again.

Progressives should fight for the budget reform principle that everybody pays a little and everybody sacrifices a little so everybody can benefit a lot. This is the way to move to the progressive center and improve the quality of life for all.

CHAPTER FOUR

Courage of Our Convictions

One evening in July 2004, I was eating dinner and watching CNN in the National Democratic Club in Washington. The news ticker was scrawling across the bottom of the screen and I began reading as the words appeared, "Congressman Charles Rangel of New York was arrested in Washington, D.C. today for . . ." I was shocked. What had Charlie Rangel done? I liked Charlie a lot. He was a smart, hardworking legislator who fought hard for Democratic policies as our ranking member on the powerful House Ways and Means Committee. Also, he was generous with his time and sage advice for younger members. Not all the Old Bulls in our Democratic caucus were as helpful, and everybody liked and admired Charlie.

But what had Charlie done to get arrested that day? It turned out that he had demonstrated the courage of his convictions for a good cause. Charlie had volunteered to commit an act of nonviolent civil disobedience to protest the ongoing genocide in the Darfur region of Sudan. In cooperation with an advocacy group, and with the prior knowledge of the D.C. police, Charlie protested on the steps of the Sudanese embassy over the failure of that government to stop the killing in Darfur. Through prearrangement with the authorities, Charlie refused to leave the embassy steps when requested and, after three unheeded warnings, was hauled off to the local police station for a brief stay, was charged with a summary offense, and paid a small fine. Most important, he reaped a lot of publicity for the plight of those being murdered in Darfur.

I learned all this when I asked Charlie about it on the floor of the House the next day. It seemed like a terrific way for a public official to draw attention to the crisis in Sudan and I wanted to follow his lead, but I knew I first needed clearance at home. I had never done anything like this before.

When I got home that weekend, my wife Francesca listened quietly to my explanation of what I wanted to do and why. She asked some questions and expressed some worries. Then she surprised the hell out of me by saying, "If you are going to be arrested for this, then so am I."

That is how it came to pass that on July 20, 2004, my wife and I got arrested for civil disobedience. We refused to leave the steps of the Sudanese embassy after polite warnings, got handcuffed, put into a paddy wagon, charged with disorderly conduct, paid a fine of $50 each, and were released. Of course, the whole process was highly choreographed and we knew there was no chance of spending the night in the slammer. But I am really proud that Francesca and I did that together.

The best part of the experience was we got arrested with comedian and activist Dick Gregory. Since the 1960s, Gregory has constantly marched, protested, and been arrested in the fight for civil rights and equal rights. While Francesca and I were doing this for the first time, Gregory said it was his 300th arrest for civil disobedience. He was pretty relaxed about it. Actually, he never stopped talking and entertaining the whole time we were in front of the embassy, in the paddy wagon, and at the police station. After we all had paid our fines and were released, the police officers and clerical staff in the station flocked around him to shake his hand and get his autograph. They recognized and appreciated a man with the courage of his convictions.

I learned a lesson that day about the importance of standing up to defend your principles and to advocate your ideas. That is what progressives have to do. Certainly, we know the importance of balance and fair-minded compromise when we fight for our beliefs, but fight we must. The public will believe in us and follow us only if we believe in ourselves.

It often seems that conservatives and right wing Republicans are tougher than progressives. They appear more willing to fight for core beliefs than we are. They certainly seem more willing and able to savage their opponents to achieve their goals.

This has got to stop. Progressives have to learn when to fight. We need both a short-term tactical plan to deal with President Trump and with the feisty right-wingers in Congress, and a longer strategy for promoting progressive ideas and success.

We should start by boldly advocating our own two-step program of balancing the budget and investing in people. We know it can be done since Bill Clinton did it. We need to have the courage of our convictions and defend our ideals. Sometimes you just have to lay it on the line.

But more is needed. In addition to fighting back with our own agenda, we progressives must acknowledge that we have some real problems. We are criticized by the right wing for being soft on national security, having weak moral values, dishonoring religion, and being too liberal on cultural issues.

Now, those accusations are bogus, but perceptions can become reality in the minds of voters, so we progressives should start by fighting back and setting the record straight, point by point.

We progressives are not soft on national security. That is a ridiculous charge. Progressive Democratic presidents have led this country valiantly in wartime and in the use of military power, from Woodrow Wilson to Barack Obama. Progressive Democratic members of Congress—to this day—vote for the money to wage those wars and fight terrorism, as do the Republicans, and we stand united in bipartisan support for our troops and our veterans.

Progressives also know that we are stronger and even safer when we work with, not against, our traditional allies and when we embrace a multinational approach to foreign policy, not the go-it-alone, cowboy diplomacy of George W. Bush or the nativist isolationism of Donald Trump.

The progressives and Democrats I know do not have weak moral values and are not disrespectful of religion. Far from it. Most of us are people of faith, just like most conservatives and Republicans. We are guided by the teachings of Jesus, Mohammed, and the Jewish prophets, just like the rest of America.

Perhaps the difference is we will not campaign, as our opponents frequently do, claiming that God favors only *our* platform and *our* candidates. And we will not use religion and religious controversies to appeal for votes, as some on the right have turned into a cottage industry.

Consider the controversy that erupted in the summer of 2010 regarding the so-called Ground Zero mosque, a proposed 13-story Islamic community center and mosque located about two blocks from the World Trade Center site in Lower Manhattan. Not surprisingly, people of good will had strong differences over this proposal. Families of the victims of 9/11 voiced both supporting and opposing opinions. Religious leaders, politicians, and the general public also expressed divided opinion. But why did some from the conservative right wing insist on adding political attacks to the mix?

President Obama weighed in to calm the waters and reaffirm the tolerant, pluralistic traditions of America. "As a citizen, and as president," Mr. Obama said on August 13, 2010, "I believe that Muslims have the same right to practice their religion as anyone else in this country. And that includes the right to build a place of worship and a community center on private property in Lower Manhattan, in accordance with local laws and ordinances."[1]

In response to that calm expression of religious pluralism, three leading conservative Republicans pounced the next day. John Boehner, the then-House Minority Leader, said, "The decision to build this mosque so close to the site of ground zero is deeply troubling, as is the president's decision to endorse it."[2] Newt Gingrich, the former House Speaker, said, "There is nothing surprising in the president's continued pandering to radical Islam. What he said last night is untrue and inaccurate."[3] My old congressional friend Peter King (R-NY) said, "President Obama is wrong . . . the right and moral thing for the President to have done was to urge Muslim leaders to respect the families of those who died and move their mosque away from Ground Zero. Unfortunately the president caved into political correctness."[4]

So, without stretching the point too far, these three leading Republicans characterized the president's calm call for religious tolerance as deeply troubling, pandering to radicalism, untrue, inaccurate, wrong, immoral, and without political backbone.

Did they really believe what they said? I doubt it. I believe they were primarily interested in using a religious controversy to score political points.

Newt Gingrich wasn't done, however, with his grandstanding, fear mongering, and divisiveness. He went on to say that building the mosque near the site of the 9/11 attacks "would be like putting a Nazi sign next to the Holocaust Museum,"[5] thus equating Islam with Nazism and coyly suggesting that all Muslims are like Nazis and are probably terrorists. Obviously, this hateful nonsense harms America's relations with hundreds of millions of peaceful Muslims around the world.

Not all Republicans were so anxious to use a religious controversy for political purposes. New York's mayor Michael Bloomberg, then a Republican, spoke clearly and admirably for religious understanding. In his defense of the mosque proposed near Ground Zero, Bloomberg declared that it must be allowed to proceed because the government "shouldn't be in the business of picking" one religion over another. "I think it's fair to say if somebody was going to try, on that piece of property, to build a church or a synagogue, nobody would be yelling and screaming," the mayor said. "And the fact of the matter is that Muslims have a right to do it, too."[6]

President George W. Bush also spoke eloquently in the days following 9/11, giving voice to the finest American traditions of tolerance and generosity. On September 17, 2001, President Bush said, "America counts millions of Muslims amongst our citizens, and Muslims make an incredibly valuable contribution to our country. Muslims . . . need to be treated with respect. In our anger and emotion, our fellow Americans must treat each other with respect . . . they love America just as much as I do."[7]

President Bush and Mayor Bloomberg's comments were courageous and inspiring, just as the demagoguery of many of their fellow Republicans was disappointing.

Nothing challenged America's tradition of religious pluralism more than the 2016 campaign of Donald Trump. On December 7, 2015, after a deadly mass shooting in San Bernardino, California, Trump issued a written statement that called for "a total and complete shutdown of Muslims entering the United States until our country's representatives can figure out what is going on."[8]

He is president now and is still shamefully using fear tactics about immigrants to rouse his political base.

Progressive Americans in both parties know that appeals to religious intolerance weaken our society and have no place in our political discourse.

Progressive Americans understand and honor the wisdom of our founding fathers that directed us to separate church from state. While that famous phrase does not appear verbatim in the Constitution, President Thomas Jefferson coined it in his famous 1802 letter to the Baptist Association of Danbury, Connecticut, in which Jefferson referred favorably to the Constitution's Establishment Clause. President Jefferson wrote:

> I contemplate with sovereign reverence that act of the whole American people which declared that their legislature should 'make no law respecting an establishment of religion, or prohibiting the free exercise thereof,' thus building a wall of separation between Church and State.[9]

That wall of separation has served America extremely well for over 230 years. Let's not tear it down now.

In addition to religious tolerance, progressives have strong moral values underpinning our entire social agenda: feeding the hungry, clothing the naked, healing the sick, housing the homeless, and caring for the elderly. These are biblical values, for heaven's sake, based upon tenets common to all religions.

We should be proud of these important traditional values. We need not cower in the face of right-wing intolerance and bluster. We should continue to defend religious tolerance and promote social policies based upon shared values. That is the way to find the progressive center in America today.

Progressives are accused of being too liberal on cultural issues and too softhearted and mushy-headed to think clearly, spend prudently, or govern wisely.

Not true. Progressives are proud of their liberalism that stems from the belief in the importance of liberty and equality. Most liberals support such fundamental ideas as national constitutions, free elections, human rights, capitalism, free trade, and the separation of church and state.

Classical liberalism developed in the eighteenth century and was based on the ideal of limited government and the liberty of individuals including freedom of religion, speech, press and assembly, and free markets. The American Bill of Rights gave these principles full and eloquent expression.

Social liberalism as developed in this country in the 20th century is the belief that classic liberalism should be tempered with social justice. Social liberals promote a robust role for the state in addressing economic and social issues such as unemployment, health care, public education, and civil rights.

Modern American progressive thought combines social liberalism, including its government spending programs and mix of private enterprise and government regulation, with liberal cultural causes including voting rights for minorities, abortion rights for women and environmental protections for all.

Modern progressivism is not too liberal for American voters, on cultural, social, or economic grounds. After all, Theodore Roosevelt's New Nationalism, Woodrow Wilson's New Freedom, Franklin D. Roosevelt's New Deal, John F. Kennedy's New Frontier, and Lyndon Johnson's Great Society were widely popular in their day. These progressive presidents found great public support for their programs of traditional social liberalism that looked out economically for the little guy, while staying out of his bedroom and promoting responsible business practices.

We modern progressives are not too liberal, representing as we do a return to the traditional social democracy of some of our greatest presidents. Perhaps, though, we are viewed as too tolerant.

We care deeply about growing and sharing the economic pie. So we champion not just the successful and well connected but also those that struggle and toil mightily every day to hold down jobs, pay their bills, and raise their families. We focus our attentions and our policies on helping working families survive and flourish in a highly competitive free enterprise system.

We also remind the country, on our better days, of our obligations to the least, the last and the lost among us. Some of those people and some of those causes are unpopular. Some of those people are poor. Some are criminals. Some reside here illegally. Some were born here with every advantage and just can't make it without a helping hand from the social safety net. Our advocacy of those people and those causes hurts us with many voters when economic times are bad.

Progressives need to keep our eyes focused on the prize of a good economy. Our liberal social views have much support in the country, but voters are most concerned about their jobs, their retirement security and their children's future. When the brutal reality of the pocketbook issues distracts the country, we progressives face the danger of losing our connection with voters who are struggling every day to get to the next paycheck. We need the courage to remind the country that our obligations to the poor cannot be ignored, while we concentrate on the pocketbook issues of working families. In fact, those obligations are stronger than ever in tough times. President Kennedy spoke often of how a rising tide lifts all boats, and the progressive movement must address the economic problems of all Americans during difficult days.

What do progressives need to do to retain political power? We must ask all Americans, particularly the successful and well connected, to pay their fair share of taxes and bear their share of sacrifices in restrained spending to get our fiscal house in order, while continuing to keep the country safe. Invest restored budget surpluses in more jobs, better public schools, and health care for all. These are the real responsibilities of government and they require our attention, not the fear mongering over abortions, guns, and gays.

My wife and I lived in a wonderful neighborhood in Abington Township, a leafy suburb of Philadelphia, for 38 years. We raised our two children there. They walked to the local public elementary school and played in the local park. Later we took our grandchildren to play in that same park. When we walked around the neighborhood, we marveled at the people we had known, the neighborhood children we saw grow to maturity, the young couples who moved in and started families, others who had come and gone, and the older couples who were aging in place as we were. We counted our blessings.

Up the street from us, a gay male couple lived for over 20 years. Around the corner, another gay male couple lived for about the same time. Both couples were friendly and good neighbors who kept a low profile. They both owned their properties and paid their taxes on time. They obeyed all the township rules and regulations. They put out the trash on the scheduled trash day and took in the empty barrels that night when they got home from work. They shoveled their sidewalks promptly when it snowed. They kept their houses in good repair and kept their yards well trimmed and well raked. They didn't have wild parties and the police were never summoned to their residences. No children were snatched from the sidewalks in front of their houses. The only way they stood out was their flowerbeds were the nicest in the neighborhood.

Those two gay couples did not threaten my marriage, my family, or my neighborhood. Actually, they strengthened my marriage, my family, and my neighborhood. If they choose someday to marry, more power to them.

I used to support civil unions for same-sex couples. When I ran for the U.S. Senate in 2004 that is what I proposed, not full marriage equality. I realize now that I was afraid of the issue and afraid of the public backlash that I believed was sure to come to any statewide candidate in Pennsylvania who favored same-sex marriage. When I ran for governor in Pennsylvania in 2010, I am glad I supported full marriage equality for same-sex couples.

Why the change? I came to understand that my marriage and my neighborhood are not threatened by gay marriage, and everyone is entitled to equality in America. I should have understood that sooner. Happily, full marriage equality is now the law of the land.

The right wing has long understood the political power of emotional distractions in public life. Although solid majorities of Americans support abortion rights, sensible gun safety restrictions and marriage equality, conservative political operatives relish beating up progressive candidates on these hot button social issues, counting upon the enflamed conservative base to work harder, donate more, and cast more votes than the complacent progressives.

But do Americans really want their national elections fought over abortion, gun safety and gay marriage, as conservative political operatives seem to think? Those issues do and should attract a lot of progressive support, but they don't define the progressive movement and we should not let the right-wingers claim otherwise. This was put into proper perspective during the 2004 presidential election when Christopher Heinz defended his stepfather, Democratic nominee John Kerry, by pointing out that progressives won't make you have an abortion, take away your gun, or turn you gay.

The power of these issues is very strong in the political process. There are many voters who proudly consider themselves single-issue voters and who cast their ballot solely based on a candidate's stand on these controversial social issues. Such single issue voting occurs on both sides of these issues and can overwhelm any other considerations.

Clearly, no advocate for or against these emotional social issues will be able to please everyone. People who care about these matters have strongly held positions rooted in both fact and emotion, and they are not likely to change their minds. The stronger you take your stand on one side of these issues, the madder the people will be on the other side.

What should progressives do? The answer is easy: stick to our guns. We have to be clear and candid about our views on the social issues. We must have the courage of our convictions.

What we should not do is pander to people, or tell them what we think they want to hear, or make promises when we don't know what the facts are. That will only get us into trouble.

Early in my career as a young state legislator, I was invited by my late friend Everett Smith to attend services at Willow Hill Community Baptist Church where he served as pastor. Reverend Smith made sure the ushers seated me in the front of the small African American church and made me feel welcome. During the service, Pastor Smith suddenly called for all the "true believers" in the sanctuary to come forward and gather around the piano for a blessing. Now, I am not given to showy public displays of my religious beliefs. But when all the people around me got up to gather around the piano, I certainly did not want to sit there alone in the pew while the rest of the church came forward. Frankly, I also wanted to impress the crowd with the depth of my faith. So I gathered around the piano with the others, and we all received a beautiful blessing from the pastor. It was not until we were asked to return to our seats that I realized that most of the worshippers had stayed in their pews—only the first two rows had come forward. My face flushed as I sensed the eyes of the congregation upon me, and I felt like a fool. I had pandered to the group and they knew it. It was a painful lesson learned.

Another time, during my first run for Congress, I committed the cardinal but not uncommon political sin of not knowing what I was talking about. The Teamsters were interviewing me in my bid for their endorsement over my opponent, the Republican incumbent. I thought the interview with seven or eight Teamsters officials was going really well and I was growing confident of securing their important endorsement. As the interview was winding up, John Morris, the legendary head of the Teamsters in the Philadelphia area, asked me in a casual way how I felt about the proposed federal deregulation of the trucking industry. Well, I didn't have a clue about the proposed deregulation. I was thinking this was something I probably should have studied before the interview, but it was too late now. I glanced at my young staffer, who was sitting against the wall, and his eyes were wide and he looked panicked. The Teamsters were all looking pleasantly at me, anticipating my answer. I had to say something. Then, with a wave of relief, I remembered that Senator Edward Kennedy was in favor of trucking deregulation. If it was good enough for Ted Kennedy, it was good enough for me, so I confidently announced my enthusiastic support for trucking deregulation.

Shocked silence was followed by general uproar. The Teamsters stared at me in disbelief, and then they all started shouting at me at the same time. Several threw their papers up in the air. John Morris was roaring at me, and I was unceremoniously escorted out of the building. My young staffer was in shock and couldn't speak. It turned out that the Teamsters opposed—really opposed—trucking deregulation. I lost their endorsement in the campaign. I learned that honesty is the best policy, particularly if you haven't done your homework and don't know what you are talking about. A simple admission that I did not know the issue, and a request for their position, would have served much better.

Frankly, if progressives want to attract public support for our candidates and our policies, we have to show some spine. If we want to influence the public debate, if we want to attract people to the progressive center, we have to tackle these tough issues with both courage and compassion. We need to speak plainly and without guile. We must also understand that we may not possess all of the wisdom in the world on these subjects.

Abortion

From the beginning of my public career in the 1970s, I have supported a woman's right to choose on the question of abortion. I trust women to make their own personal, private decisions regarding reproductive health issues. A woman and her doctor, not the government or her politicians, should decide these matters.

But there are plenty of politicians who do want the government to make these decisions. President Trump and the Republican majorities in Congress want to take away from women their fundamental reproductive freedoms. Polling has consistently shown that most Americans want abortion to be safe, legal, and rare, and progressives should lead the fight to protect these personal rights.

Every state legislature has battled over these issues since the 1973 United States Supreme Court decision in *Roe v. Wade*. The legislative battle in Pennsylvania was joined in earnest in 1981, and I was fortunate to be a state legislator then and involved in the middle of the fight.

In the Roe decision, the Court stated "a right of personal privacy or a guarantee of certain areas or zones of privacy, does exist under the Constitution . . . this right of privacy . . . is broad enough to encompass a woman's decision whether or not to terminate her pregnancy."[10]

Social conservatives in Pennsylvania as elsewhere were outraged by *Roe v. Wade* and began years of legislative actions to overturn the court decision or limit its scope and impact. These efforts came to a head in the Pennsylvania House of Representatives on December 8, 1981, when we began debate on the proposed Abortion Control Act.

The prime sponsors of the legislation were two young, conservative, true-believing Republican legislators named Steve Freind and Gregg Cunningham. While they couldn't outlaw abortion totally in Pennsylvania due to the Supreme Court decision, they wanted to limit the number of abortions in every way possible. I considered their legislative proposal to be mean-spirited, punitive, and designed to create roadblocks for women choosing to exercise their constitutionally protected reproductive freedoms.

The Freind-Cunningham legislation would require a 24-hour waiting period for women seeking abortions, permit any person to go into court to seek injunctive relief against a woman planning an abortion, require minors to have the consent of both parents for an abortion, define a fertilized egg as a human being, prohibit the use of public funds for most abortions, and prohibit private insurers from including abortion coverage in their standard policies. The legislation would impose strict new civil and criminal penalties on women and their doctors, ranging up to seven years in prison and $15,000 for violations.

The Pennsylvania House of Representatives, then and now, was divided about two-thirds anti-choice and one-third pro-choice in its voting patterns, so the small group of progressive legislators willing to fight the Freind-Cunningham proposal knew we had an uphill and almost certainly losing battle on our hands. But we were determined to fight anyway and spent several days and evenings planning our legislative strategy.

We finally settled on a plan that included procedural motions so we could challenge whether the legislation was germane, whether it violated the state constitution, and whether it should be returned to committee. We prepared a substitute amendment to transform the proposal into a "very mild regulatory act with light penalties," as described in an excellent 1982 *Philadelphia Inquirer* report written by William Ecenbarger.[11] We also drafted specific amendments to change or eliminate one by one the most offensive parts of the Freind-Cunningham proposal.

When debate started, the progressive team offered and debated our procedural motions but we were voted down on each one. I then offered the substitute amendment designed as a frontal assault on the Freind-Cunningham proposal. My amendment would have eliminated the 24-hour waiting period, abolished the private right of action for injunctive relief against women seeking abortions, changed two-parent consent to one-parent notification, dropped the provision for colored pictures of fetuses and abortions to be shown to women during the 24-hour waiting period, deleted the definition of a fertilized egg as a human being in order for IUDs and low dose birth control pills to remain legal, allowed public funding, permitted private insurance to cover abortion, and dropped most of the criminal penalties.

The Hoeffel substitute amendment got hammered, 44 yeas to 152 nays. It was too much of an assault for the small number of troops we could marshal. So our group began to offer the individual amendments, with limited success. The requirement for two parents to consent to a minor's abortion was changed to one-parent consent, in recognition of the reality that some families are nontraditional and others are plagued with domestic violence that could be triggered by such a requirement. The odious provision was dropped that would grant legal standing to anyone to seek a court order against a woman planning an abortion.

During the debate on the amendment to abolish the private right of action, I described the provision as "an invitation to every fanatic in this state who wants to take people to court, who wants to file petitions, who wants to harass women, to harass doctors, to harass clinics."[12]

Gregg Cunningham responded, "This section protects the lives of babies who are born alive when an abortion is improperly performed. Once a baby is killed or allowed to die, no legal action is going to bring that baby back to life."[13]

I believe that odd statement actually cost Freind and Cunningham some votes by raising the possibility of some wild-eyed vigilante rushing to the nearest court from a clinic or hospital to save the baby after a botched abortion. The amendment to eliminate the proposed private legal actions was approved by a vote of 137 yeas to 55 nays.

While I admired the sincerity of their beliefs, and liked them both personally, Steve Freind and Gregg Cunningham pushed things to the extreme. One of the strangest provisions in their legislation was a proposed seven-year jail term for any doctor who performed an abortion on a minor who was pregnant due to incest, without first securing the consent of the young girl's mother. While apparently intended by the legislative sponsors to improve the reporting of incest, this penalty seemed particularly strange and punitive toward the doctor since the maximum penalty for the actual incest itself was only five years in prison under existing law.

But Steve Freind was adamant. In a press conference after the bill was passed, he was asked if the legislation was intended as a message to doctors. His response, "Look, we can't stop abortions. The message we are sending to doctors is this: 'we can't stop you from performing abortions. We wish we could, and we hope to God that someday we'll get the Human Life Amendment so we can. But until that time there are going to be regulations you'll have to follow if you're going to perform abortions.' That's the message."[14]

Yes, that was the message, plus the threat of seven-year jail terms.

After two days of legislative action and debate, the bill was finally passed in the House by a vote of 132–61. I voted no. On December 15, 1981, the State Senate passed the legislation by a vote of 29–21.

On December 23, 1981, Governor Dick Thornburgh courageously vetoed the bill. In his thoughtful, carefully reasoned seven page veto message, the governor stated, "I am concerned that [some] provisions, and to some extent the entire tone and tenor of the bill, would have the effect of imposing an undue and, in some cases, unconstitutional burden upon even informed, mature adults intent upon obtaining an abortion under circumstances in which the U.S. Supreme Court has determined they are entitled to do so."[15]

The governor's veto was not the end of the abortion debate in Pennsylvania, not by a long shot. Steve Freind and Gregg Cunningham quickly regrouped and introduced a revised Abortion Control Act that was passed in the House on June 7, 1982, over my objections, by a vote of 127–61. The bill was changed enough to satisfy Governor Thornburgh and he signed it into law. There have been some legislative changes and court modifications in the three decades since, but that law essentially remains on the books in Pennsylvania to this day.

And that is the problem. Our current state Abortion Control Act remains punitive, mean-spirited, and designed to throw roadblocks in the path of women, particularly poor women and young women, who choose to exercise their reproductive freedoms. The 24-hour waiting period is an economic burden for many women who have to take off two days from work and, in some cases, travel long distances to secure competent and safe medical treatment. The mandatory court approval for young women who won't or can't secure parental consent is burdensome for the young woman and the judge. The written material and lecture delivered to the woman that is prepared and mandated by the state government smacks of Big Brother. No constitutional right should be so harassed and burdened as abortion is in Pennsylvania.

Strong opposition to abortion rights exists in every statehouse and in Congress. This dispute will continue for years to come, and abortion opponents will look for any avenue at the state or federal level to restrict and even eliminate women's reproductive freedoms. As conservative strength grows, and as the Republican Party continues to be dominated by its right wing, the battle will intensify over the essential question of who decides whether or not to terminate a pregnancy: women or politicians.

Being pro-choice means more than allowing women to control their own bodies—it also means empowering women and trusting them to make their own decisions about their personal well-being, their family security, and their economic future.

I know the right wing will continue to harass, limit, and burden reproductive freedoms every way they can. Progressives in both political parties need to wake up and not take for granted existing reproductive freedoms. We need to fight back.

Progressives must mobilize to oppose the heavy hand of government reaching ever more obtrusively into our bedrooms and our personal lives.

Guns—"Let Me Go Home"

On the evening of June 17, 1999, my friend and colleague Carolyn McCarthy delivered the greatest speech I heard on the floor of the House during my six years in Congress.

Congresswoman McCarthy represented the Fourth District of New York from 1997 to 2014. A lifelong resident of Mineola on Long Island, Carolyn had 30 years of experience as a nurse before entering politics. Her defining issue was improving gun safety laws in America, and it propelled her into politics after a terrible tragedy occurred to her family.

On December 7, 1993, Carolyn's husband Dennis and their son Kevin were riding on a commuter train on the Long Island Railroad. A crazed gunman opened fire randomly upon the unarmed passengers on the train, killing six, including Dennis, and wounding another 19, including Kevin.

Carolyn became an advocate for increased gun safety and championed that issue in her first election to Congress in 1996. She was the leading advocate in Congress for sensible, reasonable regulation of firearms. Among other gun safety issues, Carolyn led the fight for better regulation of gun shows.

Gun shows have become controversial in the United States as public safety advocates and many in the law enforcement community consider the shows a source of illegally trafficked firearms. Gun advocates, especially the National Rifle Association, believe that their Second Amendment rights are being jeopardized by any attempt to regulate gun sales at gun shows. While federally licensed gun dealers are required to conduct instant background checks at their stores on gun purchasers, this does not apply to private sellers of guns at flea markets or gun shows. This provides convicted felons, domestic abusers, substance abusers, and other prohibited purchasers with an opportunity to evade background checks, as they can easily buy firearms from private sellers at gun shows with no accountability or oversight.

On June 17, 1999, the House was debating HR 2122, the Mandatory Gun Show Background Check Act. The legislation proposed to establish background checks at gun shows but had been weakened by an amendment that limited the waiting period to 24 hours and provided for automatic approval of the gun purchase if the background check couldn't be completed in those 24 hours. Gun safety advocates believed the legislation as amended lacked teeth and needed a longer waiting period, so Carolyn offered her amendment to extend the waiting period to three days for completion of the background check.

The battle lines were drawn and the debate raged for and against the amendment for the allotted 30 minutes. Carolyn was the last to speak on her amendment, and here are her verbatim remarks, in their entirety, delivered off the cuff and from the heart, without any notes:

> Mr. Chairman, I thank all of my colleagues for their support. This is very hard for me tonight. It is hard for me because I have heard so many different things. I have been here just about three years and I am used to all the different spins. I do not understand them all the time, but that is what I do.
>
> What we were supposed to be doing tonight was trying to serve the American people. What we are doing tonight is saying and listening to the victims across this country. That is all we are trying to do. That is the only reason I came to Congress.
>
> Someday I would like to hopefully not have to meet a victim and say I know, because it is really hard. We have heard the arguments on both sides, and I wish we had more time to really say the truth about everything. My amendment closes the loophole. That is all I am trying to do.
>
> I am trying to stop the criminals from being able to get guns. That is all I am trying to do. This is not a game to me. This is not a game to the American people.
>
> All of my colleagues have to vote their conscience, and I know that. But I have to tell my colleagues, mothers, fathers, who have lost their children, wives that have lost their loved ones, this is important to them.
>
> We have an opportunity here in Washington to stop playing games. That is what I came to Washington for. I am sorry that this is very hard for me. I am Irish, and I am not supposed to cry in front of anyone. But I made a promise a long time ago. I made a promise to my son and to my husband. If there was anything that I could do to prevent one family from going through what I have gone through and every other victim that I know have gone through, then I have done my job. Let me go home. Let me go home.
>
> I love working with all of you people. I think all of my colleagues are great. But sometimes we lose sight of why we are all here. I am trying to remind my colleagues of that.

Three business days, an inconvenience to some people. It is not infring-ing on constitutional rights. It is not taking away anyone's right to own a gun. I do not think that is difficult for us to do. If we do not do it, shame on us, because I have to tell my colleagues, the American people will remember.[16]

Carolyn McCarthy had held the rapt attention of the House during her powerful speech, which was unusual for any speaker, let alone a mere second-termer. She received a standing ovation from every member on the floor when she finished, which virtually never happened. She was flushed with emotion and energy, and her friends in the House were thrilled for her. We applauded and cheered her loudly.

But they didn't let Carolyn go home that night. The McCarthy Amend-ment went down to defeat, 193 yeas to 235 nays.[17] The entire House was willing to stand and applaud Carolyn McCarthy that evening for her per-sonal sacrifice and for her principled stand on guns, but a majority was not willing to stand up to the National Rifle Association, which opposed the McCarthy Amendment and had lobbied the members against it.

That is what you need to know about the politics of guns, and many other social issues, in America. No matter how good the cause or moving the speech, people so often seem to have their minds already made up on the subject, or simply follow the dictates of a pressure group. If we are ever to make any real progress on gun safety or a host of other hot button social issues, we do need to find reasonable and rational ways of approaching these challenges.

All Americans of all political persuasions were horrified by the at-tempted assassination of Congresswoman Gabrielle Giffords and the senseless murders and shootings in Tucson, Arizona, in January 2011. Nobody but the insane shooter himself was responsible for that terrible violence. But sensible people also know that it is time for America's leaders to tone down the excessive political rhetoric and strengthen the gun safety laws that keep us safe.

We should no longer tolerate the violent imagery and provocative lan-guage of some of our political leaders. I hope we have heard the last of Sarah Palin's "lock and load" rhetorical flourishes and her website targeting of opponents' districts with gun sight crosshairs.[18]

Progressive leaders across the country must fight to strengthen the laws to keep guns out of the hands of criminals and the mentally ill.

A great place to start is with Everytown for Gun Safety, an advocacy group founded in 2014.[19] They seek to educate the public about the con-sequences of gun violence and promote efforts to keep guns out of the hands of criminals. The group supports background checks for all gun sales and laws that prohibit domestic abusers from obtaining firearms. They support safe gun storage mandates and strengthening penalties for gun trafficking.

These are all sensible, rational and reasonable proposals. Any one of them would make America safer against gun violence. None of them impinges one iota on the Second Amendment and the legitimate constitutional rights of law-abiding citizens to buy, own, and legally use firearms.

Gun advocates, gun rights organizations, conservative lawmakers, and a lot of hunters who totally distrust their elected government are opposing these sensible proposals, lobbying against them, introducing legislation to deny them and filing lawsuits to block them.

But we must soldier on. We are in for a battle, and we know that our communities will be safer with the enactment of reasonable gun safety rules.

We need to stand up for elected officials willing to take political risks for us. The opponents of gun safety measures are relentless. The National Rifle Association never sleeps, refuses to compromise and will oppose the reelection of any elected official who merely seeks common ground between the warring sides in any controversy over gun rights.

The politicians who are willing to fight for reasonable gun safety measures are leading the way to the progressive center in American politics.

Gay Rights

Senator Barry Goldwater of Arizona had this to say about gay Americans serving in the armed forces, "You don't have to be straight to fight and die for your country, you just have to be able to shoot straight,"[20] and "Everyone knows gays have served honorably in the military since at least the time of Julius Caesar."[21]

Social conservatives, and all of us for that matter, could learn a lot from Barry Goldwater, the father of the modern conservative movement in America. Goldwater served for 30 years in the U.S. Senate as a Republican from Arizona. He was the Republican nominee for president in 1964, and retired from the Air Force Reserve as a Major General. He was flinty, outspoken, and a strong economic conservative who relentlessly fought what he perceived to be the evils of American liberalism. Senator John McCain, his successor in the Senate, said of Goldwater in 1994, "He transformed the Republican Party from an Eastern elitist organization to the breeding ground for the election of Ronald Reagan."[22]

Barry Goldwater also supported gay rights. Late in life he became quite outspoken about it. He was offended by the increasing influence of the Christian right on the Republican Party. Goldwater's libertarian principles could not abide the attempts of the religious right to impose their morality on America and he rebelled, speaking up for gay rights and abortion rights, and against mixing religion and government.[23] We would be better off today if some of the self-appointed arbiters of morality in America understood and channeled some of the social tolerance of Barry Goldwater.

There is much more legislative work to be done in Congress and the state legislatures to afford equal rights and equal protection to gay Americans. Discrimination based on sexual orientation and gender identity still exists in the country. Extending full civil and legal rights to gay Americans is the next great civil rights challenge facing all of us.

One of the stupidest laws Congress ever passed was the federal Defense of Marriage Act that defined marriage as a union between a man and a woman. The law denied federal benefits to any couple that did not meet this description.

It is a mystery why Congress ever thought it was a good idea to deny federal benefits to same-sex couples. After all, those couples pay federal taxes and are American citizens. Why should a union of two loving people of the same gender be repudiated and be subjected to discrimination by the federal government?

Section 3 of the Defense of Marriage Act defined marriage for the purposes of federal law as a union of one man and one woman. It was unfair to gay Americans to deny them the benefits and responsibilities of legally sanctioned marriage and seemed to be a violation of the equal protection and due process clauses of the Fifth and Fourteenth Amendments to the Constitution. It took a while to resolve the constitutional issues, but the U.S. Supreme Court finally ruled in 2015 that Section 3 violated the Fourteenth Amendment and struck down the law.[24]

One of the great accomplishments of Congress in 2011 was the repeal of "don't ask, don't tell," the ban on gay people serving openly in the military. That policy was a compromise initiated by President Clinton in 1993 after his failure to completely repeal the ban on gays in the military. Under the policy, military recruiters were not allowed to ask about sexual orientation, but if a military service member acknowledged they were gay, they were dismissed from the service. The policy never resolved the fundamental unfairness of banning gay men and lesbians from openly serving in the military, and it resulted in over 13,500 dismissals from the military services of gay Americans who just wanted to serve their country.

President Obama promised during his campaign in 2008 to end the policy and he was able to win broad support from Democrats in Congress and enough moderate Republican votes to avoid a filibuster in the Senate and pass the repeal in 2011. Military surveys indicated that most people in uniform do not object to serving side by side with gay soldiers, and public opinion polls showed most Americans wanted to end the ban.[25]

More protections are needed. We should make sure that every state law against hate crimes includes crimes based upon sexual orientation and gender identity and expression. This would give local and state prosecutors more authority and more tools to investigate crimes that are based, in whole or in part, on anti-gay bias and hatred and would make it easier for the law enforcement community to bring such perpetrators to justice.

The federal government has already accomplished this milestone in gay rights. On October 28, 2009, President Obama signed into law a measure that makes it a federal crime to assault an individual because of his or her sexual orientation or gender identity.

The federal hate crimes measure was named for Matthew Shepard, a gay Wyoming teenager who died after being kidnapped and severely beaten in October 1998, and James Byrd Jr., an African American man dragged to death in Texas the same year. President Obama hailed the hate crimes provision as a step to "help protect our citizens from violence based on what they look like, who they love, how they pray."[26]

The United States Supreme Court has greatly expanded legal rights and protections for gay Americans since 1996. Landmark rulings have allowed homosexuality to be protected as a class in state and federal law, struck down sodomy laws, ruled that marriage embraces more than just one man and one woman, and at long last made same-sex marriage legal.

But the federal government still has no comprehensive anti-discrimination law protecting lesbian, gay, bisexual, and transgendered Americans. Discrimination continues in housing, employment, medical facilities, and other legal relationships in various ways among the states. President Trump and right-wing politicians are even willing to deny transgendered students the right to use the school bathroom of their choice. More work must be done to apply tolerant attitudes, progressive values, and full equality to these challenges.

Martin Luther King said, "The arc of the moral universe is long but it bends towards justice."[27] America still has a long way to go before all Americans are treated fairly and equally no matter their sexual orientation, but we have made great progress. We are bending, we are leaning, and we are moving in the right direction.

Controversies surrounding abortion rights, gun safety, and gay rights will be challenging us for a long time. We must understand two things: our positions on these issues must be clear and we will not be able to please everyone. Progressives must show tolerance, wisdom, and courage. If we do, the American people will follow our political leadership, even if they don't agree with us on every particular detail of every issue.

What the people want is leadership, and the progressive movement must be prepared to give it to them. The fact is that we embrace, just like conservatives, the beauty of individual liberty and the economic magic of the free marketplace. But unlike the right wing, progressives also believe in public action for public good. We know we are all in the same boat. We see government as a necessary and positive force that, when properly used, will improve the quality of everyone's life.

Let's face the facts, fix our mistakes and fight like hell. We need to listen to the voters who sometimes reject our message. We need to sharpen that message to respond to the real concerns of Americans, not to the spin of the other side. And we need to believe in our message and in ourselves.

Oliver Wendell Holmes Jr., the influential writer and thinker who served for 30 years on the United States Supreme Court, urged all Americans to lead lives of action and passion. In an 1884 Memorial Day address in Keane, New Hampshire, Holmes said, "I think that as life is action and passion, it is required of a man that he should share the passion and action of his time at peril of being judged not to have lived."[28]

Surely, the progressive movement has an equal obligation to embrace the challenges of the Age of Trump with action and passion.

If progressives respond to the demands and the hopes of the public marketplace with simple authenticity and passionate conviction, if we can attract more Americans to the progressive center, then we will be able to get things done for the American people.

CHAPTER FIVE

Medicare for All

I learned much from my father on the subject of national health-care reform. Dad was a doctor and practicing surgeon until he retired at age 65 and lived a full and happy life until he died at 86. He was a lifelong critic of socialized medicine, and opposed Medicare when it started in the mid-1960s. But over time his views changed.

No domestic issue has inspired, challenged, and bedeviled our elected national leaders in recent years more than national health-care reform. President Obama and the congressional Democrats passed the Affordable Care Act into law, and now President Trump and the congressional Republicans are repealing it. But the fundamental problems of who is covered for which services at what cost have not been solved to the satisfaction of most Americans.

So what do we do about improving our health-care system?

Dad's lifetime experience, and the lessons I have drawn from his career and my own experience, teach me that our best solution to the health-care challenge is to pursue seven guiding principles to establish Medicare for All. Let me explain by starting with his story.

Both of my parents were born and raised in Wisconsin and came to the East Coast as young adults with those traditional Republican values that we associate with the small town Midwest of the last century: pay your bills on time, stay out of debt, keep your nose out of other people's business, be tolerant of the foibles of your neighbors, and fight like hell for your family and your country.

Mom and Dad, like millions of others, expected their government to reflect those personal virtues as well. While not active politically, their traditional values caused them to fully embrace the Republican Party. Dad was such a traditional Republican that he believed until his dying day that Richard Nixon had received a raw deal.

When I came home from college in the summer of 1972, I was a big supporter of George McGovern for president. I had marched in several Vietnam War protests in Boston in 1971 and 1972, and I was an enthusiastic student volunteer for McGovern that spring during the Democratic primaries. In fact, I was then proudly holding my first political office— cochair of Boston University Students for McGovern—and I thought I knew everything there was to know about politics.

Dad, of course, was rabidly rooting for the reelection of President Nixon. Our dinner conversations that summer became so heated that Mom quickly banned all political discussions at the dinner table. So Dad and I kept the debate going by clipping newspaper editorials that supported our candidate and leaving the clippings on each other's pillow—the liberal *New York Times* supplied me with lots of editorial fodder in favor of McGovern while the then-conservative *Philadelphia Inquirer* kept my Dad well stocked with pro-Nixon commentary. We kept the scissors furiously clipping all summer—but no minds were changed.

My father wasn't always the conservative defender of the establishment that he seemed to be when I was growing up. One of his favorite stories was about the time when he was an undergraduate student at the University of Wisconsin in the late 1930s. It seems that the progressive governor, Philip La Follette, had proposed a cut in state funding for the university and the students didn't like it. So Dad and his friends mounted a protest march on the Capitol that ended up with Dad standing on the desk of the Governor's receptionist and getting mud all over the letters she was typing. The governor agreed to speak to the students and that was the end of the protest. In later years, Dad couldn't remember if the spending cut was restored or not. For the rest of his life he felt guilty about his muddy shoes forcing that secretary to redo her typing, but he was always particularly proud of his Day of Protest.

The best part of the story happened about 25 years later. Mom and Dad were on a cruise to Bermuda and recognized former governor La Follette and his wife in the bar. Dad dragged Mom over to their table, made the introductions and established their common Wisconsin roots, which pleased the La Follettes. Dad complimented the former governor on his political career, which ended in 1939, and there were broad smiles all around. Then Dad excitedly recounted the last time he had seen the governor in person, which was from the vantage point of the receptionist's desktop. At that point, Governor La Follette abruptly rose to his feet, took his wife by the hand and announced, "Isabel, we are going in to dinner," and they marched off to the dining room. That was the end of that budding friendship. You have to love a politician with a long memory.

When Medicare started in 1965, my sister and I were teenagers living at home. I remember clearly how upset my father was about Medicare. He was then in his forties with a booming surgical practice, and he honestly believed that the advent of Medicare was the start of socialized medicine in the United States. Dad believed that the federal government would soon employ all the doctors in the country and own all the hospitals, just like the socialized medical system he detested in Great Britain. He actually visited my sister's high school to engage in a debate in front of the students about Medicare and he took the position that Medicare represented the beginning of the end of American health care as we knew it.

Despite my father's personal opposition, Medicare was established in 1965. Within a couple of years, Dad's views had changed. He noted with approval that for the first time in his medical practice all his older patients were suddenly able to pay their bills. The payments provided by Medicare weren't as high as other insurers were paying in those days, but at least he was receiving a reasonable fee for his surgical services. He liked that. He really liked that he no longer had to charge other patients more to cover the unpaid bills of older patients who simply couldn't pay, and he no longer had to cope with worried adult children and the spouses of those older patients who were frantic about paying those bills. He realized that seniors were no longer delaying or even refusing needed surgery because they couldn't pay. And, lo and behold, he was still an independent medical provider practicing at a community-based, nonprofit hospital. The government was paying the bills of the older patients without employing the doctors or owning the hospital.

I believe that the success and necessity of Medicare was the beginning of my father's political awakening. Make no mistake, he stayed a loyal Republican for many more years and always had that soft spot for President Nixon. But both Dad and Mom began to see the big picture politically and began to embrace the notion that there is a legitimate need in many parts of our society for public action for the common good.

Truth be told, it was Newt Gingrich that pushed my parents over the political edge. With their traditional, Midwestern Republican values, they simply couldn't stomach Gingrich's brand of intolerant, confrontational, hyperpartisan government in the 1990s that valued tax cuts for the rich over fiscal responsibility. And my mother was kind of fond of Bill Clinton.

So my parents in their early eighties changed their party registration to Democratic; Mom a year or two before Dad. And they were both registered

Democrats when they died, which to this day remains the most astonishing political development of my life.

My parents got it right. I believe, as they came to believe, in public action for public good to improve the quality of people's lives. The most effective way to improve the quality and delivery of health care and the most efficient way to cover all Americans is to institute Medicare for All.

Health Care: Problems Remain

We are all familiar with the problems that challenged health care in America before the Obama presidency. Costs soared, far more than the negligible increase in personal incomes. Those who already had health insurance worried that their own costs would be forced up by any reform plan to cover the uninsured. Paperwork, pre-approvals, and bureaucratic overhead clogged the health-care system—most primary care physicians were forced to have more clerical help in their offices than nursing support.

Our country was spending more than twice as much per person on health care as the other industrialized countries. We were not getting demonstrably better health results than other wealthy countries such as Canada, France, and Japan, although insurance companies, drug companies, and large hospital systems were enriched.

Few people were happy with our health-care system, not the doctors who provided the care or the patients who received it or the employers who largely paid for it.

Clearly, reform was needed.

The great health-care debate of 2009 resulted in the Patient Protection and Affordable Care Act, passed by Congress with no Republican votes, and signed into law by President Obama in March 2010, which promised to cover more Americans, hold insurance companies accountable, lower health-care costs, guarantee more choice, and enhance the quality of care for all Americans.

Portions of the law took effect immediately that put an end to some of the worst insurance company practices. No longer could insurers cancel coverage for people who are sick, or deny coverage for those with preexisting conditions, or limit the amount of lifetime coverage. Insurers must provide free immunizations for children and free preventive care such as mammograms. Young adults could now remain on family health plans until they turn 26, an economic blessing both to young adults and their families.

The biggest mystery for me of the 2010 election is why so few of the Democrats who passed the Obama health-care reforms were willing to take credit for it during their reelection campaigns. After putting up with all the outright lies about the health-care bill, while it was under consideration, like Sarah Palin's outrageous claim that "death panels"[1] would be established to deny care and pull the plug on Granny, you would think the supporters would have loudly promoted their success in reining in the insurance giants. But few Democrats running for reelection to Congress in 2010 talked about health care at all, even though those worthy insurance reforms became law just six weeks before Election Day.

Progressives always need to have the courage of our convictions. We must be willing to defend our records, and define and explain our accomplishments. If we don't, the right wing will do it for us, and we know how distorted that will be. If we believe in something, we better be willing to fight for it.

Lyndon Johnson said, "What convinces is conviction. You simply *have* to believe in the argument you are advancing; if you don't, you are as good as dead."[2]

It is even worse if you won't advance your arguments in the first place. The failure of congressional Democrats to promote and defend their historic passage of health-care reform allowed the right wing to demagogue on the issue and to demonize the bill's supporters. Progressive Democrats created a vacuum in the public debate over health care that the right-wingers were happy to fill.

They have filled that vacuum with a lot of nonsense. Former Virginia attorney general Ken Cuccinelli, on the subject of the Affordable Care Act, said that if Congress can force a private citizen to buy health insurance then federal officials could "order you to buy a car. Order you to buy broccoli."[3]

Attorney General Cuccinelli fits into a long line of prominent conservatives who has made outlandish claims about progressive proposals that never came true. Here is a sampling, thanks to an article in the *New Republic* in 2009:[4]

> The child will become a very dominant factor in the household and might refuse perhaps to do chores before six a.m. or after seven p.m. or to perform any labor.
> —*Senator Weldon Heyburn (R-ID), in 1908, on why*
> *child labor should remain unregulated*

> [I]t would make it practically impossible for any publisher in the United States to accept any food, drug or cosmetic advertising without facing squarely into the doors of a jail.
> —*Federal Trade Commission Chair Edwin L. Lewis, in 1935, on the*
> *dangers of empowering the Food and Drug Administration*
> *to regulate the food, drug, and cosmetic industries*

[The Act represents] a step in the direction of Communism, bolshevism, fascism, and Nazism.
>—*The National Association of Manufacturers, in 1938, condemning a national minimum wage and guaranteed overtime pay*

It is socialism. It moves the country in a direction which is not good for anyone, whether they be young or old. It charts a course from which there will be no turning back.
>—*Senator Carl Curtis (R-NE), in 1965, opposing Medicare*

Right-wing zealots continue to make outrageous claims to try to debunk progressive ideas, and we have to stand up and defend our proposals and our achievements and not abandon the battlefield to the Sarah Palins and Ken Cuccinellis of the world.

The Affordable Care Act was not perfect, but it did contain important reforms that expanded coverage and reduced costs, benefiting the previously uninsured and those with inadequate, substandard policies. And it survived a tortured review by the U.S. Supreme Court.

The Affordable Care Act was ruled constitutional by the Supreme Court in a highly anticipated and controversial decision, *National Federation of Independent Business v. Sebelius*, on June 28, 2012, in a 5–4 vote.[5] The key question before the Court was whether Congress had the constitutional authority to require citizens to engage in commerce by mandating the purchase of health insurance.

It is not unusual for state and local governments to require certain commercial activity, such as the legal mandate in many states that drivers must buy automobile insurance. But until the Affordable Care Act, the *federal* government had never mandated that individuals throughout the country engage in a certain commercial activity, such as buying health insurance if they did not already have it, or paying a penalty for failure to comply.

I thought the individual mandate in the law was a proper exercise of the power Congress is granted in the Constitution to regulate commerce. Many times the Supreme Court has approved regulatory acts of Congress regarding business practices as appropriate under the Commerce Clause of the Constitution.

But the Court had never before approved a congressional act *requiring* certain commercial activity, or *penalizing* commercial inactivity, and it was not certain that the conservative Roberts court would extend the Commerce Clause powers far enough to validate the Affordable Care Act.

And the Court did not. Only the four "liberal" Justices (Ginsburg, Breyer, Sotomayor, and Kagan) believed that the individual mandate was permitted under the Commerce Clause. The five "conservative" justices (Roberts, Scalia, Kennedy, Thomas, and Alito) believed the individual mandate exceeded the powers of Congress and was thus unconstitutional.

But, astonishingly, the matter did not end there. Chief Justice Roberts apparently decided that the Affordable Care Act needed to be upheld. He surprised the legal world by deciding that the financial penalty included in the Affordable Care Act for failure to comply with the individual mandate was not actually a penalty at all, but was a *tax*, and as such was permissible under the Constitution. The four liberal justices quickly agreed with the Chief Justice, and the Affordable Care Act was upheld by a 5–4 vote.

Certainly, there is no question under the Constitution that Congress has the power to levy a tax. But there is a huge question whether the financial penalty in the Affordable Care Act is truly a tax. I believe it is a penalty, a fee, or a sanction that must be paid if the individual refuses to comply with the mandate to buy insurance. A tax is a payment that applies broadly to all people who are similarly situated. Everyone with income pays the income tax. Everyone who owns property pays the property tax. Everyone who buys something pays the sales tax. But how could the chief justice state with a straight face that a financial penalty that only some people pay for failure to comply with a mandate is actually a tax?

Here is what Chief Justice Roberts said in his opinion, "The Affordable Care Act's requirement that certain individuals pay a financial penalty for not obtaining health insurance may reasonably be characterized as a tax. Because the Constitution permits such a tax, it is not our role to forbid it, or to pass upon its wisdom or fairness."[6]

His characterization that a financial penalty is actually a tax does not seem reasonable at all to me. And while I am not surprised that the four liberal justices agreed with him in order to provide the votes to find the law constitutional, I don't know how they could justify it either. I am very glad the Affordable Care Act was upheld, but the reasoning of the Court was unsound. The Supreme Court should apply common sense and reasonable legal standards when they do their work.

The fact of the matter is the Affordable Care Act worked well to provide better coverage and health care to millions of Americans. The government's list of good outcomes due to the law is impressive.[7]

Over 20 million Americans accessed quality, affordable coverage for the first time through private plans and expansions in Medicaid and the Children's Health Insurance Program. The law gave these families real financial security because insurance companies could no longer deny them coverage because of a preexisting condition or because they reach an annual or lifetime limit in coverage.

Insurance companies were required to spend at least 80 cents of every premium dollar they received on health care—rather than things like marketing or profits.

Prescriptions were more affordable for seniors by phasing out the Medicare donut hole.

The life of the Medicare Trust Fund was extended by 13 years.

Millions of young adults received coverage under their parent's plan, because the law says they can now do so until they turn 26.

Seventy-six million Americans with private health insurance could finally get preventive services such as vaccines, cancer screenings, and yearly wellness visits without cost sharing, because the law says insurance companies must provide these services with no co-pay or other out-of-pocket expense.

These were all very good things. President Trump and the congressional Republicans will ultimately be punished politically if their plan to replace the Affordable Care Act does not match these accomplishments.

But neither Obamacare nor Trumpcare goes far enough to truly reform health insurance and improve health care for all Americans. To achieve those goals, we need a single-payer health-care system modeled on Medicare that is publicly financed, administered through a public-private partnership, and privately delivered by medical providers.

Health Care: The Impact of Money

The United States Congress and the Clinton and Bush Administrations talked a lot about health care during the six years I served in Congress from 1999 through 2004.

Some reform proposals were passed into law during this time, most notably adding prescription drug coverage for seniors to Medicare. Other key issues were neglected, primarily the pressing need to provide all Americans with health insurance coverage.

Why did some high-profile issues receive legislative attention and presidential advocacy during this period, resulting in a new law like prescription coverage in Medicare, while other critical reforms like universal health insurance continued to languish?

During this time, 45 million seniors were enrolled in Medicare, while 46 million other Americans had no health insurance. Seniors wanted prescription coverage and the uninsured wanted health insurance. Seniors got what they wanted and the uninsured did not.

Why did the political system in Washington, D.C. during this period work for one large group of Americans but not for another equally large group?

The reason is money, the impact of money in the political process. The difference is the pharmaceutical industry and the American Association of Retired Persons (AARP) used their clout to lobby in favor of drug coverage in Medicare, while the health insurance industry used its clout to oppose universal health insurance.

Seniors had the big pharmaceutical companies with big lobbyists and big bucks on their side, and the result was legislation granting a new, privatized drug benefit to Medicare. This allows the pharmaceuticals to market their new insurance plans for drug coverage to those same seniors, with lots of public Medicare dollars to underwrite those private plans and private profits.

The pharmaceutical manufacturers reinforced their furious lobbying for a privatized drug benefit in Medicare with generous political donations to the campaigns of the politicians who supported them.

The numbers tell the story. According to the OpenSecrets website of the nonpartisan Center for Responsive Politics, the pharmaceutical manufacturers greatly favored Republican congressional candidates and incumbents over the Democrats during this period. In the 1999–2000 election cycle, the pharmaceuticals donated $6,566,433 to Republicans and $2,860,566 to Democrats. By the 2003–2004 cycle, the disparity in donations had grown to $9,074,974 for Republicans and $4,816,309 for Democrats.[8]

The pharmaceutical industry put most of their political money and muscle behind the Republican Party that was favoring the industry's legislative position. Campaign contributions flowed in large amounts to Republican incumbents, candidates, and party campaign committees, coupled with aggressive lobbying by representatives of each pharmaceutical company as well as Pharma, the industry trade association. All this money and muscle succeeded in enacting a prescription drug benefit to the industry's liking.

And what was happening at the same time to enact universal health insurance for the uninsured?

The uninsured had an advocate in the White House. Bill Clinton was serious about extending health-care coverage to all Americans. He made universal health-care coverage a centerpiece of his administration in 1994 with a stirring speech to Congress devoted to the subject, and he put a smart, capable, and tough woman named Hillary Clinton in charge of developing the program. The Clintons really meant business.

And we all know what happened. The Clinton plan, dubbed "Hillary-Care" by her detractors, was devised in secrecy, appeared top heavy and too bureaucratic, and ultimately was defeated by the health insurance industry, which feared losing its stranglehold over health-care coverage.

The industry spent heavily on the "Harry and Louise" television ad campaign that was designed to scare the daylights out of Americans regarding the future of their health care under the Clinton plan. The multimillion dollar ad campaign convinced most Americans that they would lose the ability to choose their own doctors and hospitals if "HillaryCare" was approved. Those fears were unfounded, and the industry's claims were untrue, but there was no big ad campaign from the plan's advocates to counter the fear mongering of the health insurance industry. So, the public was misled and political support for the Clinton plan collapsed.

The uninsured have no big industry behind them like the pharmaceutical companies and no big, self-interested lobbying group like AARP on their side. So the uninsured struggle for attention and assistance.

The pharmaceutical companies are making some very big bucks under Medicare. The Bush administration drug plan, for the first time, diverted billions of Medicare dollars away from payment for medical services and earmarked the money instead for private drug company profits. Additionally, the Bush plan specifically prohibited the federal government from negotiating with the drug companies for lower prices on pharmaceutical drugs, even though the Veterans Administration does negotiate with the drug companies and accordingly pays considerably less than Medicare for prescription drugs on a per unit basis. No wonder those drug companies were delighted to lobby for this legislation and to give their campaign donations to legislators who supported it.

During this time, President Bill Clinton and congressional Democrats wanted to establish a prescription drug benefit in traditional, publicly supported Medicare that would cover all drugs approved by the Food and Drug Administration and prescribed by a physician. We also wanted to require Medicare to use its huge bargaining power to negotiate lower drug prices with the pharmaceuticals, saving money for seniors and the government. But the majority congressional Republicans blocked this until President George Bush took office and gave administration support for the partially privatized drug benefit in Medicare favored by the drug industry that was finally passed into law in late 2003.

Under the new law, identical Medicare services and benefits are no longer available to all Americans. The numerous private plans being offered with large public subsidies vary widely state by state. While the new Medicare prescription coverage is available to all Americans in some form or another, discrepancies exist across the country.

There is simply no good reason why the seniors in some states, all good Americans and U.S. taxpayers, should not get the same Medicare options and services as seniors in the rest of the country. Medicare is a federal program, available for over 50 years on the same basis to all older Americans no matter where they live. Privatizing the new drug benefit and other medical coverage is breaking faith with that long-standing national commitment we have with each other to provide the same health-care coverage to all older Americans.

Congressional Republicans now want to change the way the federal government pays the health-care bills of seniors. Currently, Medicare makes direct payments to doctors and hospitals when bills are submitted for medical care provided. Medicare does this with administrative costs of about 2 percent of program expenditures, according to the Kaiser Family Foundation.[9] The Republicans want to change to a voucher system where Medicare would pay a set amount per senior directly to private insurance companies for health-care coverage.[10]

This GOP plan would be a gift for health insurance companies that currently receive no payments for traditional Medicare coverage. They would start receiving federal payments that they would use in part to cover their advertising costs, bureaucratic overhead, and private profits. But taxpayers and seniors would suffer. Federal tax dollars would be buying less health care for seniors, as some of those existing dollars would be skimmed off the top to compensate the private plans. Seniors would receive less health care and more uncertainty, as the health-care vouchers would be designed to increase in value at a slower rate than health-care costs actually would be rising. The private plans with new public subsidies would flourish, while seniors and taxpayers would get squeezed with less coverage and more red tape.

Privatizing Medicare is not the answer. We need to take the success of traditional Medicare and expand it.

Medicare for All

It is clearer than ever before that Bill and Hillary Clinton were fundamentally correct when they identified the lack of health insurance coverage as the biggest failure of American health care, and the problem is bigger today and costing us all more money than when the Clintons tried to fix it in 1994. President Obama's health-care reforms were beneficial and were working but did not go far enough. Now, President Trump and the Republican Congress are moving backward by repealing Obamacare without an adequate replacement.

American health care has several serious problems, and the lack of coverage for millions of Americans is just one of them. The findings of numerous recent studies and surveys indicate that Americans are spending more and getting less for their health-care coverage.

The United States has traditionally spent over 30 percent of our total health-care costs on administration. That is hundreds of billions of dollars every year on bureaucracy, paperwork, profits, and overhead.

Canada has a publicly supported "single payer" health insurance system where the government collects the taxes and premiums necessary to provide health care for all Canadians, then proceeds to pay the bills submitted by private doctors and hospitals. Canadian administrative health-care costs for their provincial single payer system are under 2 percent, according to a study published in the *New England Journal of Medicine*, compared to 31 percent administrative overhead for U.S. private health care, 3.6 percent for Medicare and 6.8 percent for Medicaid, the state-federal health-care program for low income Americans.[11]

Granted, Canadian-style single-payer health insurance has some significant challenges, like issues of rationing services and treatment delays. But the system is consistently popular in public surveys and is considerably more efficient than our complicated insurance system with all our forms and clerks and red tape.

According to a 2015 report by the Organization for Economic Cooperation and Development, 10.2 percent of Canadian gross domestic product was spent on health care, which covered 100 percent of Canadians, while 16.4 percent of U.S. gross domestic product was spent on health care, which covered just 84 percent of Americans.[12]

Single payer health care in Canada is not socialized medicine but is a social insurance system that is publicly financed and publicly administered but privately delivered. Only doctors in Canada make medical decisions. Compare that to the United States, where medical decisions are effectively made by both doctors and insurance companies.

Can you imagine how much more health care we could pay for and provide to sick and needy Americans if we could direct our excessive administrative costs away from red tape and private insurance profits and toward better health care for all?

In 2003, I attended a health-care conference in Florida sponsored by the John F. Kennedy School of Government of Harvard University. During one of the panel discussions, I made the point from the floor about the U.S. spending about 30 percent of health-care costs on administration while Canada, with their efficient single-payer system, was spending much less on overhead, about 10 percent I thought. A woman jumped up on the other side of the room and proclaimed, "That's not true!" The moderator politely informed the unknown woman that she was challenging a sitting United States Congressman, who presumably knew what he was talking about and would she care to identify herself and elaborate on her comment? The woman sweetly replied that she was the national administrator of the Canadian health-care system, and their administrative costs weren't 10 percent but actually were less than 2 percent. I meekly sat down and listened to her very persuasive discourse on the merits of the single-payer system covering all Canadians.

The current Medicare program has some problems and needs reform, particularly if we are going to expand its reach. As President Trump has correctly advocated, we should fix the prescription drug benefit so Medicare is required to negotiate with the drug companies for lower prices. We should reduce costs through more efficient delivery and coordination of benefits, by eliminating duplicate and unnecessary tests, and by relying on treatments proven to work best. Current Medicare Advantage plans are heavily subsidized by the taxpayers and cost more per person to deliver similar services than traditional Medicare—about 15 percent more. They must be scaled back.

We should strive for a system of universal health-care coverage—publicly financed, publicly/privately administered, privately delivered—with the following seven guiding principles:

1. Everyone is covered, and everyone contributes based on ability to pay. There is no free ride and no free lunch. Financial responsibility requires consumers of health care to pay a modest "fair share" to discourage unnecessary use.

2. Public responsibility is mandated, with accountability for costs, quality of care, and value of services. Medical providers who abuse the system are identified, punished, fined and, as a last resort, excluded.

3. No discrimination in coverage is permitted due to type of illness or ability to pay. No exclusions for preexisting conditions, no lifetime caps.

4. Coverage responds first to medical need and suffering, rather than spending caps. Universal budgeting will require economies and produce savings.

5. Payments are triggered by the quality, not the quantity, of medical service, and are outcome based. Medical providers are paid fairly and promptly, and malpractice recoveries are streamlined.

6. Simplified administration and good bargaining with medical providers minimizes financial waste.

7. Emphasizing public health, prevention, and strong primary care minimizes clinical waste.

It is high time that we insure all Americans for their health-care needs and we do it in the most efficient and socially responsible way possible, with a reformed, universal, and publicly supported system. Such a Medicare for All health plan would improve health care for all Americans, while reducing costs to America. Such a plan—socially liberal and fiscally responsible—would place our health care in the progressive center of American politics.

CHAPTER SIX

It's Broke—So Fix It

It begins about 9:30 A.M.

Any earlier and you might not find anybody at their desks or willing to talk.

By 9:30 A.M., you have chatted with your staff, read the morning papers, and scanned the online news services for the latest political scoops. You have also gulped some coffee and eaten some junk food, which you will continue to do throughout the day.

You have said good morning and thank you to any volunteers in the office, you have checked the final figures from the day before, wincing a bit that all that effort didn't result in more commitments, and you have resolutely ignored the glares from the finance department staff who wanted you to start at 9:00 A.M.

But now it is 9:30 and you can't put it off any longer. It is time to go into the call room, close the door, sit down at the table, take the first of hundreds of call sheets from your finance staffers, pick up the phone, and make the first fund-raising phone call of the day. And it won't stop until the close of business that day.

You are running for Congress. You have spent the majority of every day of the campaign raising money, and unless you have reached the last weekend of the general election you will spend the majority of every remaining day of the campaign doing the same thing. You will call family and friends. You will call business associates and professional acquaintances. You will call people you hardly know who have a history of making political donations. You will call total strangers. You will ask all of them for money.

In most cases, you will make multiple calls to the same people. You will leave many messages and numerous voice mails. Some people will be cordial and polite and will indicate they want to help you. Some will duck your calls, some will have their secretaries screen your calls, some will take your calls and say no, or will say they haven't committed to anyone yet, or they are for the other guy, or they think you are a jerk and wouldn't give you money in a million years.

Some will put their check to your campaign in the next day's mail, or will overnight it to you, or will walk it over to your office, or will drop it off that night at your house.

Some will readily make a commitment to support you and promise a check but will actually send it only after you have called back five times. Some will make their commitment but then never send their check at all, no matter how much you follow up. And all of these people, your friends and the people you thought were your friends, the saints and the sinners, will be on your call sheets in the future and you will call them all again and again for more money until the campaign is over.

And then, win or lose, you may need to call them once or twice more for help retiring your campaign debt. After that, if you plan to run again, you will call them again to get ready for your next campaign. Welcome to modern politics.

The American political system is broken.

Public elections are awash in floods of private money. Candidates and incumbents spend far too much of their limited time begging private donors and special interests for campaign donations, and far too little time meeting with the public and studying public policy issues.

Most congressional districts have been gerrymandered into safe, one-party districts where the public no longer enjoys the benefits of competitive general elections between the candidates of opposing parties with contrasting views. Instead, incumbents in those safe seats worry only about losing primary elections to competitors in their own party who pander more successfully to the extremes in each party's base. As a result, those incumbents are forced to cater to the fringe voters of their own party and are encouraged while in office to fight with the other party and avoid bipartisan compromise at all costs.

It's broke, so let's fix it. The progressive movement has long championed campaign reforms and election law improvements, and a disenchanted public is demanding reform and change. I believe the most important single thing we could do to improve our politics and our government is to end the political gerrymandering of congressional districts. We also face significant challenges in making government more transparent, ending no-bid contracts, and expanding public financing of campaigns.

The Curse of Gerrymandering

"Don't worry, Joe, I will give you a district you can run in."

This assurance came from John Perzel, then Speaker of the Pennsylvania House of Representatives, during a phone conversation we had in early 2001 to discuss what plans the Republican Speaker might have for the upcoming reapportionment of Pennsylvania's congressional seats, which would take effect for the 2002 election.

Pennsylvania, as a result of the 2000 national census, was slated to lose two congressional seats to other parts of the country that were growing faster in population than my state. The word was out that Perzel and the Republican legislators in the majority in Harrisburg, with the support of Republican governor Tom Ridge, were going to reapportion the congressional map with two goals in mind: guarantee that the two lost seats would be districts with Democratic incumbents and create as many safe Republican seats as possible.

As a Democratic congressman in a traditionally Republican seat in the suburbs of Philadelphia, I was worried, and John Perzel knew it. I had worked hard from the beginning of my political career to build support and win votes as a moderate-to-liberal Democrat in a moderate-to-conservative Republican community. I knew it would not be hard for creative and partisan Republicans to split off some Democratic areas of my district, or to add some Republican voting areas, or both, to make my re-election campaign in 2002 very difficult. Or they might just obliterate my current district from the map by combining it with another, making my reelection virtually impossible. I did not want my congressional career to end at the hands of the GOP mapmakers.

So John Perzel was promising me that they would not wipe out my current district, but apparently would give me a fighting chance to run for a third term in a redrawn district. I knew John Perzel to be a man of his word, but he would not specify his exact plans for my seat, the Thirteenth Congressional district of Pennsylvania. It turns out that he kept his word to me, but in the process devised a diabolical plan that combined the seats of two Democratic incumbents in such a way that favored the election defeat of both Democrats, one in the primary and the other in the general election, thus trying to knock out two Democrats from Congress with the elimination of just one seat.

Here is how the plan was designed to work. Representative Bob Borski, my longtime friend from our state house days together, was in his tenth term representing the Third District of Pennsylvania in Congress. Bob's seat was wholly within the city of Philadelphia and bordered my seat in suburban Montgomery County. Bob's seat had a majority of Democratic voters and mine a majority of Republicans. First, the Perzel redistricting plan combined our two seats so that Bob and I would have to run against each other in the primary, thus assuring the loss of one Democrat from Congress. Second, Perzel carefully drew the map so that a majority of the Democrats in the new seat lived in Philadelphia in Borski's current seat, which would give Bob the advantage in the primary. But a majority of all voters in the new district lived in Republican Montgomery County, giving a suburban Republican candidate a real advantage over a Philadelphia Democrat in the general election. Obviously, the Perzel plan was designed to cause me to lose the primary to Bob Borski, then Bob to lose to a suburban Republican in the fall election, thus knocking two Democrats out of Congress.

The plan did not work, but only because Bob Borski decided he had enough after 20 years of distinguished service in the House. Bob retired instead of running in the primary, served out the remainder of his term, started his own successful lobbying business, and never looked back. I was unopposed in the primary of 2002 and won a close general election with 51 percent of the vote.

Speaker Perzel used state-of-the-art gerrymandering in 2001, combining computer technology and voting data down to the neighborhood level, to attempt a highly partisan redistricting that would favor Republicans as much as possible. The fact that he did not succeed in removing two Democrats from office by combining their two seats into one does not diminish the boldness or the cynicism of his use of the dark arts of the gerrymander. In fact, the Perzel plan worked overall to favor the Republicans mightily in the 2002 election.

Because of the population shifts recorded in the 2000 national census, Pennsylvania's congressional delegation shrank from 21 seats to 19 seats to be filled in 2002. At the start of the 2002 campaign, 11 Republicans and 10 Democrats filled those 21 seats. After the 2002 election in the newly drawn districts, 12 Republicans and 7 Democrats filled the 19 seats. This was a very significant increase for the GOP and was particularly notable because it happened even though the Democrat at the top of the state ticket that year, Ed Rendell, won nearly 54 percent of the vote for governor. The Republicans running for Congress did so well, even though the statewide Democratic standard bearer won an impressive victory, because the congressional redistricting map was a partisan gerrymander.

What Pennsylvania Republicans achieved in the 2001 redistricting, they perfected 10 years later. After the 2010 census, Pennsylvania lost another seat and was down to 18 congressional seats. The Republicans once again conducted a partisan gerrymander when they drew the new districts, and the results of the 2012 congressional election were 13 GOP winners and 5 Democratic winners. This extraordinary Republican margin in the congressional delegation was not the result of Pennsylvania suddenly turning Republican. In fact, that year Barack Obama received 52 percent of the vote in Pennsylvania, and 52 percent of the voters statewide supported the Democrat running for Congress in their districts.

This unbalanced partisan split in the congressional delegation occurred because the Republicans once again drew up a redistricting map that spread Republican voters into as many districts as possible, while packing Democratic voters into as few districts as possible. The election results of 2012 show how well the Republicans did their partisan work: the 13 Republican victors won the general election by an average of 57 percent of the vote, while the 5 Democratic victors won by an average of 78 percent. This clever but cynical manipulation of voting trends and mapmaking allowed the creation of congressional districts where 13 Republicans could win comfortable general election victories, while only 5 overwhelmingly Democratic seats were established.[1]

Of course, all this packing of voters into districts to achieve partisan advantage produces a congressional map that is filled with meandering seats that wander geographically all over the place to pick up certain neighborhoods based on how they vote. The districts are not compact, do not keep communities together, do not respect municipal or natural boundaries, and just do not make any common sense.

Partisan gerrymandering is bad for our politics and our government. Voters feel estranged from their congressional representative. Incumbents don't have to worry about making difficult bipartisan decisions or seeking legislative consensus but only need to tend to their party's base to assure an easy reelection. Hardly any general elections are competitive and no politician is rewarded for trying to find common ground.

This broken system of drawing new congressional seats could be fixed easily by mandating new standards that would guide the mapmakers and reduce the partisan influences on the process. Some states have done so by requiring that congressional districts be drawn as compactly as possible, or without considering where incumbents live. Others have set up nonpartisan procedures and have taken the decision away from the elected state legislators. Other states, like Pennsylvania, require the redistricting plan to pass the state legislature and be signed by the governor like all other legislation.

Whatever method is used, it is clearly time for sensible national standards to apply to the redistricting process to eliminate the partisan abuses of gerrymandering. Unfortunately, it is highly unlikely that today's Congress, flushed with partisan fever, could ever come to agreement on a set of nonpartisan rules to guide redistricting around the nation.

It is time for the United States Supreme Court to wake up and do its job. A clear and courageous decision by the Court could quickly put an end to the evils of gerrymandering.

In several decisions in recent years, the Supreme Court has set forth a number of standards that could be applied to the process of redrawing congressional seats. Unfortunately, the Court has not mandated that states follow these standards, except in two instances.[2]

First, the Court has ruled that congressional districts within each state must be as equal in population to each other as possible—the "one man, one vote" standard—so that each citizen's vote is worth as much as another. Second, districts must be contiguous, so that no district has an outlying "island" or unconnected part. Both of these court mandates make sense.

The Supreme Court has carefully enforced these two rules by throwing out state plans that violate them, and requiring the states in noncompliance to redraw their plans.

But these two standards are not enough to prevent states from engaging in the most outrageous gerrymandering abuses. As long as the congressional districts are the same population and are internally connected, the Court does not seem to care how illogically those districts may be drawn. It is time for the Court to enforce the other sensible standards for redistricting that it has suggested but never mandated.

The Court should mandate that congressional districts be compact, respecting municipal and natural boundaries. New maps should contain the fewest possible splits in voting precincts. Communities of interest should be contained in the same district as much as possible, and new plans should preserve the cores of prior districts.

It would only take the rejection of one state's redistricting plan by the Supreme Court for violation of these rules to effectively and quickly stop gerrymandering abuses across the country. Of course, such legal challenges only make their way to the Supreme Court every 10 years, if at all, following the latest decennial census.

Congress at any time could enact the necessary reforms to apply prospectively to the next redistricting cycle. Such public-minded reform is blocked, though, because so many incumbents owe their seats and easy general reelections to gerrymandering abuses in their home states.

Gerrymandering hurts American politics and must be stopped. Progressives need to demand change. In our democracy, the voters are supposed to pick the politicians, not the other way around.

Running for Office

I ran for office 16 times starting in 1974. That year, in my first race for the Pennsylvania House, I raised $5,000. In my 2004 race for the U.S. Senate I raised $5 million. During my career I made tens of thousands of fund-raising phone calls and raised over $13 million.

The individuals I asked for money hardly ever asked for anything in return, at least not anything that would make a direct financial difference to them. They did not seem to expect that their donation entitled them to anything or gave them any special power over me. They generally agreed with my political thinking and legislative agenda and were interested in helping me win election to continue to pursue our mutual goals. This is also true, for the most part, for the organizations and special interests that I solicited for support. In most cases, we were already in agreement over a shared agenda and they were supporting me in recognition of our mutual legislative efforts.

Over the course of my political career, I have heard just about every possible response a fund-raiser can receive. About two-thirds of the political money I raised came from individual donors. Virtually all of my friends and longtime supporters were friendly and gracious whenever I called, and they almost always tried to help. Sometimes, though, my sudden inability to get past their secretaries or several unanswered messages gave me a pretty clear message that even the most loyal donor was tapped out and not willing to give again, at least not for awhile.

There is a secret to effective fund-raising on the telephone; stop talking. Obviously, you must be friendly and persuasive while you quickly share the good news about your campaign, and it is very important to listen to whatever your prospect may say so you can respond appropriately. It is best to ask for a specific dollar amount or extend an invitation to a particular event. But, after you clearly and firmly make the "ask," the final thing you absolutely must do is stop talking. Just shut up. If there is silence on the line, don't fill it. Make the prospect say something. He may say no. He may hem and haw. He may enthusiastically agree to donate at the level you requested. He may start negotiating a lower level of involvement. But I guarantee that eventually he will say something. Silence is your friend because it forces a decision. If you don't shut up, you may never close the deal.

The political action committee (PAC) directors and lobbyists represent-ing the thousands of special interests looking for favorable governmental treatment are never shy about pursuing their employer's best interests. They are paid to promote the agenda of the groups they represent, to ask public officials to support that agenda, and to report back to the groups about who is helpful and who is not. That combination of advocacy and score-keeping, with reelection campaigns always just around the corner, can result in bad judgments and poor decisions by elected officials, special interest lobbyists and campaign donors that undermine the integrity of public life.

Through the years, I raised about one-third of my campaign money from PACs. Some of my PAC donations came from organizations rep-resenting issue-oriented special interests, such as liberal, environmental, small business, and women's groups. Most of my PAC money came from organized labor, through its member unions. Big Labor, so scorned by the right wing and many business interests, actually has a comprehensive leg-islative agenda of broad importance to their members, their retirees and, generally, to all workers in America. Organized labor lobbies for univer-sal access to health care, better funding for Social Security and Medicare, more educational opportunity and economic development, and against privatized government and unfair tax cuts for the wealthy. Big Labor does not have a narrow, self-interested agenda, and I was always proud to sup-port the organizations that represent working men and women in this country.

Now, it makes little sense in a campaign to argue that the PACs sup-porting one candidate are inherently better or worse than the PACs sup-porting the opposing candidate. Voters don't much like PACs, except for the ones fighting for them. There is not a lot of political mileage to be won by bashing the other guy for being under the control of his PACs, since such tactics only invite counter claims against you and your PACs.

But, frankly, I always did believe that my PACs were better than my opponents' PACs that support the Republican Party, conservative business interests, and right-wing groups. My PACs cared about progressive issues and helped the little guy and fought for those who do not have equal power in the political or economic arenas. Their PACs, representing the corporate worlds of industry, insurance, banking, and manufacturing, just always seemed to be about making more money for themselves, through special appropriations, regulatory relief and tax breaks.

The political system has careened out of control at the state and fed-eral level in recent years, with many accusations of unethical and illegal lobbying, political money laundering, obstruction of justice, cronyism, corruption, and cover-up. A lot of public officials, donors, and lobbyists have been indicted, and many are in jail.

Clearly, private money and special interests have a huge and corrupting influence on our public life and elections. Any attempt to win back public confidence in our political system must be dedicated to the proposition that once we recognize and understand that corrupting influence, we can fix it.

The corruption I perceive is less a matter of individual dishonesty, although sadly that obviously exists, but more a result of a tainted and compromised system. No PAC director, labor official, or individual donor ever asked me to break the law or do anything improper or unethical in exchange for a donation. My guess is the other side's PAC directors and donors don't routinely do that, either.

Not many politicians break the law or act unethically when they fund-raise. It is a very stupid politician who explicitly offers his or her vote in exchange for a campaign donation. It is simply illegal to promise to take any government action in response to receiving campaign support.

Any fund-raising politician who is tempted to cross the legal line, or even come close to it, should remember this simple rule: never say anything in a phone conversation, or type anything in an e-mail, that would embarrass you if you saw it on the front page of the local newspaper. Just assume every phone conversation is bugged, and every e-mail will be leaked.

What politicians do offer donors and lobbyists is access and attention. Public officials remember who supports their campaigns, and their big donors stand out and get extra attention. I once gave a quick, off-the-cuff answer that was more revealing than I initially realized to a college student's question about whose phone call I would return first from a big pile of messages. I answered, "My wife, the press, a donor, a campaign worker, a constituent I know, then constituents I don't know, in that order." I was trying to make the point that eventually I return all my calls, but I must admit that donors ended up pretty high on the list.

Most individual politicians are not corrupted by specific donations, but the political process clearly is corrupted by the pervasive culture of giving and receiving campaign cash. The collective decision-making of public officials at all levels of government is adversely affected by the influence of private money given through the political process and lavished on the system through gifts, favors, golf trips, and the like. The more selfish the goals and generous the donations of the special interests involved, the more attention the political process will pay to those special interests, and the more the average citizen and taxpayer will be ignored.

There are many examples in recent years in both political parties of the corrupting influence of private money on public life. Clearly, pay-to-play government contracting is hurting public life, when public officials allow campaign contributions and personal favors to influence the hiring of professional vendors like lawyers, engineers, architects and other consultants needed for public projects.

Politics can be nasty and unforgiving. The stench of pay-to-play corruption fouls the public image of everyone associated with the practice, guilty or not.

When I was a reform candidate for county commissioner in my suburban Republican county in the 1990s, I called it the Court House Culture: the assumption by the governing Republicans then in power that the county personnel office was the private hiring hall for the county GOP. They specialized in patronage hiring, no-bid contract awards to GOP cronies and donors, and general favoritism in county government decisions.

It was called "Bush cronyism and corruption" when George W. Bush was in power, as national Democrats objected to similar failings in Washington, D.C., and the country was treated to numerous charges of insider trading, influence peddling, political money laundering, criminal conspiracy, leaking the identity of a covert CIA agent, and lying to the FBI.

Donald Trump promised throughout his campaign for president to "drain the swamp" in Washington, D.C. Clearly, that was one of his most popular election promises. The country is watching to see if President Trump succeeds, or if merely a new bunch of cronies and supporters start feeding at the public trough in place of the previous bunch. Progressives need to hold the president accountable.

Lord Acton was right about power leading to corruption,[3] and nothing corrupts the system faster or more absolutely than money. And he would not be impressed by the weak attempts taken so far to reform our campaign finance laws that just seem to spawn new ways for private money to flow into the public arena.

What should we do? First, make sure government is open and accountable, while still able to function. Second, stop the abusive practices of no-bid contracting and use competition to save tax dollars, and safeguard the public interest. Third, reduce the influence of private money on public elections with full disclosure of donations and expanded use of public financing for campaigns.

If we can advance this reform agenda, if progressives can display our belief in the importance of government by fighting hard to clean it up, then we can restore the tattered faith of many voters in the honesty and integrity of the political process. That is the way to lead people to the progressive center of American politics.

Increase Government Transparency

Open and transparent government is a very good thing and needs to be continued and expanded. Various Sunshine and open records laws have been passed at all levels of government in recent years giving reporters and private citizens improved access to government records and decision making. These requirements for public decisions to occur in public, not behind closed doors, can cramp the style of politicians but clearly serve the greater public good of openness and accountability.

But politicians still have to be able to talk privately, gather information, discuss ideas, and kick things around with each other. Good legislation at any level of government is invariably the product of a lot of back and forth discussion, private negotiation and horse-trading, along with public input, fact-finding, and open debate.

Pennsylvania has a good open meeting law, the Sunshine Act,[4] which I supported in its earliest versions, when I was a young state legislator in the early 1980s. It requires that government meetings be open to the public and forbids a quorum of any governmental body from taking any official action in private or deliberating in private for the purpose of reaching final decisions. The state courts sensibly have ruled that any private decisions that may be reached, inadvertently or not, by government officials do not violate the Sunshine law if the issue in question is subsequently decided with a recorded vote at an advertised public meeting with full opportunity for the public to be heard.

I strongly support open government. So imagine my frustration when I found myself in a controversy over the Sunshine law in 2010. A local newspaper reported with great fanfare that Commissioner Jim Matthews and I regularly met for breakfast at a local diner during our service as the bipartisan governing coalition on our three-member Board of County Commissioners. The newspaper had us virtually tried and convicted of a Sunshine law violation in their breathless coverage, even though Jim and I protested that we did not decide anything at these breakfasts. Further, decisions by the Pennsylvania appellate courts specifically permit elected officials to have private conversations or conduct inquires about government business as long as actual deliberations and final action occur only at a subsequent advertised public meeting.

But our protestations of innocence and explanations of the law fell on the deaf ears of the editor of the *Norristown Times Herald*, who was convinced he had a hot scoop.[5] His overheated and inaccurate coverage led the county district attorney to start an investigation and convene a grand jury. But the inquiry into "Breakfastgate" came up empty and wasted a lot of public resources. No Sunshine law violations were found or charged by the DA or the grand jury. Frankly, I still believe that the powers-that-be in the county seat, including the self-described "partisan Republican" newspaper editor and the ambitious Republican district attorney, simply were trying to smear my Republican colleague Jim Matthews any way they could in punishment for his decision to form a governing coalition with a Democrat.

There is no question that the press is doing its job when it holds public officials accountable for their actions. There is an old saying that what is important about a free press is not that it is accurate, but that it remains free. I agree. But the media really needs to keep working on the accuracy part, too.

Congress and state legislatures have exempted their own Republican and Democratic party caucus meetings from most open government requirements, while granting public access to legislative committee meetings and floor debates and mandating debate transcripts and recorded public votes. I support keeping party caucuses private, although I know that frustrates open government advocates.

In eight years of Democratic caucus meetings in the Pennsylvania House and six years in Congress, I never heard any unethical or unlawful things discussed, contemplated, or proposed. Instead, the caucus meetings give the party leaders the opportunity to discuss the issues of the week, both legislative and political, and give the sponsors of bills a forum to promote and explain their legislation. Rank-and-file members have an opportunity without public attention or embarrassment to ask questions or express doubts about a particular bill or the party's program. Candid discussions, fact finding, and opinion sharing among legislators will not happen if the press is there to report on every dumb question or blunt conversation.

But it is very important for all official action to occur in public with adequate notice, public input, recorded votes and accountability. Such transparency will serve and protect the public interest.

Because of their privacy, these caucus meetings can be pretty entertaining. Distinguished elected officials don't hesitate to crack jokes, swap insults, and freely express themselves, often in very colorful language.

One time in the early 1980s, the Pennsylvania House Democratic caucus was holding a private evening meeting during budget season, after an afternoon voting session and a dinner break. One of my colleagues from Philadelphia rose to his feet to comment on a bill scheduled for a vote later that evening when the House returned to public session. The bill proposed new state regulations for private nursing homes and my friend perceived the legislation as a threat because his family had financial interests in the nursing home industry.

So far, so good. No problem for my friend to express his opposition to the bill, based upon his experience and his family's financial interest, which he freely and openly acknowledged. The good part came when he pulled his handwritten remarks from his pocket and began his presentation. He proceeded to deliver a vigorous, angry, scathing denunciation of the proposal and everyone associated with it, laced with some magnificent profanity. He put swear words together in combinations I had never heard before. He read every word of his obscenity-laced tirade that was all written down on his crumpled piece of paper. No doubt, he had used the dinner break and the aid of a few drinks to prepare his commentary. Never before or since have I heard anyone actually use a prepared text to read a string of curse words.

Another time in the mid-1990s, the Democratic caucus of the U.S. House was privately discussing a bill to lower the legal limit for blood alcohol levels for drivers from .1 percent to .08 percent. The private debate swirled back and forth with advocates saying Congress needed to act to make the nation's highways safer from drunk drivers, while opponents worried that the proposed limit was too low and would ensnare safe, otherwise law abiding drivers. Finally, one of my Pennsylvania colleagues representing coal country who seldom spoke in the caucus stood up to oppose the bill and said, "You can't do this, it would be unfair to my people back home. My district wakes up at .08."

Despite the colorful language and occasional frat boy humor, party caucuses serve an essential function in the legislative process by allowing frank discussion and candid consensus building. Let the politicians talk in private, then require them to vote and explain themselves in public, in the bright sunshine, and hold them accountable. The public servants should answer to the public, not the other way around.

End No-Bid Contracting

Our next goal should be to end contracting abuses and pay-to-play scandals. The best way to do that is to eliminate no-bid contracts. We should require every public contract with a professional or consultant to be subject to competition. If professional advisors are required to compete for government business, they will sharpen their pencils and offer their best services at their best price, generating the best value for the taxpayers.

Most states and the federal government already require competitive bidding under strict requirements for the purchase of goods and the awarding of construction contracts. These laws require the selection of the lowest responsible bid, with few exceptions. In fact, if a higher bidder can prove that the "lowest" bidder for a contract actually fudged the numbers or violated procedures, the government can be forced to throw out the tainted bid and give the award to the second lowest bidder, or start the bidding process over. This statutory process works well where it applies, and it screens out any influence from friends or donors.

Professional service contracts are handled differently, and for good reason. The lowest price simply should not be the only requirement when a government body is hiring a lawyer, engineer, architect, or other professional. Actual experience, prior performance, and knowledge of the assignment are equally important to the hiring government as the amount of the professional's fee.

But that doesn't mean that professional contracts should be handed out without competition on a "no-bid" basis. That allows appointments to be influenced by favoritism and cronyism or, almost as bad, the appearance of favoritism and cronyism. Equally important, most government contractors, no matter how ethical and professional, will not offer their lowest price unless forced to do so through a competitive process.

The hiring body has the best chance to arrive at the best value for the taxpayers if it issues Requests for Proposals and solicits competitive responses from qualified professionals.

The reform benefit of using Requests for Proposals and other competitive processes is clear. Even if a proposer is a campaign donor or personal friend of the politician doing the hiring, the competition will require all proposers to put their best foot forward at their best price. And the hiring authority has written responses not only to evaluate but also available to justify the hiring decision if challenged later on. No more private handshake deals when spending public money to hire private contractors.

I learned long ago that the competitive process works in the best interests of government. In 1992, I was a new Montgomery County commissioner with two other colleagues also new to the job. We needed to issue a General Obligation bond to borrow money for the county's ongoing capital program. The year before, the prior county administration had done a comparable borrowing of similar size and had appointed without any competition a well-regarded, highly qualified Philadelphia law firm, Ballard Spahr, to do the bond work, for which the firm requested and was paid $55,000. When we needed to borrow the following year, the three of us decided to use a competitive process to choose our bond counsel. We issued a Request for Proposals to a number of law firms that were qualified to do bond work. Most of the proposals we received were considerably less than the fee the county paid the previous year. We decided not to accept the lowest priced proposal because the responding lawyer did not have a lot of experience doing bond deals and was not familiar with Montgomery County. Next lowest price was our old friend Ballard Spahr, who obviously had sharpened its pencils and proposed to do virtually the same competent legal work with the same well-qualified lead bond lawyer as it had performed the year before, but this time for a 50 percent lower fee of just $27,000. There was no question that using the competitive process resulted in the best value for county taxpayers.

Make the professionals compete and sharpen their pencils. It is the only way to get a good price from the prospective vendor and the best value for the government and the taxpayer.

Reform Campaign Finances

Our third goal should be full disclosure of campaign donations and more reliance on public financing of elections, to reduce the inevitable corruption of public campaigns by private dollars.

Unfortunately, we are moving in the wrong direction on this reform agenda at the national level. Recent federal elections have seen a tsunami of undisclosed corporate and special interest donations flood the nation's airwaves paying for nasty attack ads. This occurred due to a truly unwise 2010 Supreme Court decision as well as lax tax laws covering nonprofit organizations. Congress must act to correct this situation if voters want to know who is paying for the negative TV ads that dominate political debate in this country.

We haven't seen so much secret corporate spending on political campaigns since the days of President Nixon right before the Watergate scandal. Nixon's reelection campaign, grandiosely named the Committee for the Re-Election of the President (and aptly described by the acronym CREEP), was raking in large and undisclosed corporate and individual donations just before a new campaign finance law was due to take effect on April 7, 1972. Common Cause got wind of all the secret contributions and sued to require disclosure of the list of donors, which was maintained by Rose Mary Woods, Nixon's secretary. The list soon came to be known fondly as "Rose Mary's Baby." Common Cause was successful and the list of secret donors was disclosed,[6] and the favoritism, corruption, and illegality that became apparent caused great public outcry and directly led to the Watergate reforms that define that era in presidential politics.

Today, special interests and individuals with private agendas are still giving campaign money secretly, now at levels far higher than previous elections, but it is all legal. President Trump and Congress must legislate new reforms to drain the political swamp and restore sanity to our national politics.

In *Citizens United v. Federal Election Commission* in January 2010, the Supreme Court's 5–4 conservative majority relaxed decades of restrictions on corporate and union spending on political campaigns. Ruling that the First Amendment permits unlimited third party spending on campaigns, the court majority stated, ". . . we now conclude that independent expenditures, including those made by corporations, do not give rise to corruption or the *appearance* [emphasis added] of corruption . . . [T]he appearance of influence or access (to elected officials), furthermore, will not cause the electorate to lose faith in our democracy."[7]

The great columnist E. J. Dionne put it well when he told his readers, "You can decide what's more stunning about this statement, its naivete or its arrogance."[8]

I am as appalled as Mr. Dionne by the Supreme Court's decision. It is obvious that unlimited and undisclosed special interest spending is precisely what causes the appearance of corruption. And my experience with the voters indicates that the mere *appearance* of special interest influence and access to politicians is exactly what causes the public to lose faith in democracy.

In this particular case, the Supreme Court majority simply had no idea what they were talking about. They could not have been more incorrect.

President Obama swiftly blasted the court's decision, saying "the Supreme Court has given a green light to a new stampede of special interest money in our politics. It is a major victory for big oil, Wall Street banks, health insurance companies and the other powerful interests that marshal their power every day in Washington to drown out the voices of everyday Americans."[9]

House Republican Leader John Boehner of Ohio called the decision "a big win for the First Amendment" as long as donors disclose every dollar they spend on campaigns. "Let the American people decide how much money is enough," he said.[10]

But that is the problem. The American people cannot determine who is making all the donations. Not only does the court decision allow special interests to spend freely on political campaigns, but lax tax laws and weak regulations governing campaigns allow the big corporations to give their millions to sympathetic nonprofits who are not required to disclose their donors. These nonprofits have patriotic sounding names, but the public or national interest is the furthest thing from their minds.

The nonprofits use these secret special interest dollars to do the political dirty work of the corporate and special interests. No disclosures are necessary, so no accountability is possible. The public airwaves become a target-rich, no-risk political shooting gallery where the special interests can attack and smear candidates without responsibility or fear of public backlash.

Congress must act to change the law and limit the damage of what is, intentionally or not, an extraordinarily political decision by a court that is not supposed to be political. Our national political system had reached a rough parity in recent times, a balance of power between the two major parties and their backers that resulted in competitive and close presidential elections and changing majorities in Congress. That healthy and robust competition is threatened by the lopsided impact on our campaigns of unlimited and undisclosed corporate dollars.

Full disclosure of all political donations would go a long way to correct the problem. It shouldn't be so hard to impose such requirements, since we are coming from a reform period where such disclosure was the norm.

It is much tougher to bring openness and sunshine to a system that is long used to operating in the dark. In June 1977, in my first term as a state legislator, the Pennsylvania House debated my bill to require pre-election disclosure of campaign finances. Believe it or not, at that point Pennsylvania law merely required state and local candidates to publicly report their campaign fund-raising and spending 30 days *after* an election. It was a mystery to me how that post-election disclosure was of much benefit to the voters, who did not have access to that information before they went to the polls. So I proposed legislation to add a 10 day pre-election disclosure to the reporting requirements.

All the young reformers in the House thought this was a great idea. But the day we reviewed the bill in the closed-door Democratic caucus, all hell broke loose. The old guard was outraged. It was bad enough they had to disclose their donors and spending after an election, but they sure didn't want to do so beforehand. Why give a political opponent or hostile press any ammunition right before Election Day? Two of my veteran colleagues from western Pennsylvania, A.J. "Gus" DeMedio and John "Jackie" Brunner, got so mad at me during the caucus that they had to retire to the Speaker's Office next door to get their blood pressure checked. But the good government types—disparaged as "Goo Goos"—prevailed and the full House passed the bill the next day. Gus and Jackie were good men and stalwart Democrats who were in public service because of a sincere desire to help people. They just weren't keen on letting people know what they were up to regarding their campaign finances before Election Day. We got along well after the caucus fireworks, although they always referred to me afterwards as "that Goo Goo."

In addition to full disclosure of all campaign contributions, we need to expand the use of public financing and other "clean elections" reforms to reduce the outsized impact of inside players and huge donations in our politics. Public financing in presidential elections was started as a Watergate-era reform and has worked very well over the years, providing financing on a matching basis for campaigns in both primaries and general elections paid for by a voluntary check off on federal income tax returns. In reality, several recent presidential campaigns have rejected the public funding because the candidates were confident, with good reason, they could raise more privately than the public financing would provide their campaigns. It would be a very good idea to raise the total amount of public money that major-party presidential candidates are entitled to for their general elections, so that more candidates would opt in.

Under a clean elections system, candidates wishing to receive public financing would collect a certain number of small qualifying contributions from registered voters. Once enough donations are received, the candidates then receive a flat sum from the public financing pool to run their campaigns, and agree not to raise any other money from private sources. Candidates who are outspent by privately funded opponents may receive additional public matching funds.

One potential vehicle for progressives to use to limit the impact of the *Citizens United* ruling is legislation called the Fair Elections Now Act introduced in the Senate by Senator Richard Durbin (D-IL)[11] and previously in the House by my friends Reps. John Larson (D-CT) and Walter Jones (R-NC).[12] It aims to allow candidates to opt in to the system to run for congressional office without relying on large contributions, big money bundlers, or donations from lobbyists, through a formula where small contributions qualify candidates for fixed public payments and reduced media broadcast rates. Two of the options available to pay for this public financing of congressional elections could be a small fee on large government contractors, or 10 percent of revenues generated through the auction of unused broadcast spectrum. However we pay for public financing, it is a worthwhile reform that would clean up our national politics.

I must tell you more about my two former colleagues in the U.S. House. Walter Jones is one of the fine Southern gentlemen in Congress, soft spoken, courtly, unfailingly polite, and a man of deep faith. For two years, I was fortunate for my office to be located next to Walter's in the Cannon House Office Building on Capitol Hill. Walter is a conservative

Republican who was a strong supporter of President George W. Bush and his Iraq war policy, at least at the beginning. But Walter lost faith in the president and came to view our invasion of Iraq as a tragic mistake. Soon after the war started, Walter began to place poster boards on tripods in the hall outside of our offices with the names and photos of the American soldiers who were dying in Iraq. As the casualties mounted the poster boards became more numerous, soon filling the spacious hallway with a grim, sad, and very moving reminder of the human toll being exacted by our policy in Iraq. People would just stand in the hallway, gazing reverently at the posters. Walter received a lot of criticism for his respectful but jarring display of the war dead and was subjected to significant pressure from his party to take down the posters. But Walter never wavered. He didn't grandstand or lose his courtly composure. He just let the names and photos speak for themselves.

John Larson is a charming, gregarious liberal pol from Hartford, Connecticut, with more than a touch of Irish blarney. John and I were freshmen together in 1999 and he rose quickly in the House leadership due to his mastery of policy and politics. One evening in our first term in Congress, we met by chance at a popular Capitol Hill restaurant. I was hosting my new office staff for dinner after a day of training, and as John walked by our table I introduced him to my team and asked him to favor us to a sampling of his famous imitation of Senator Ted Kennedy. John immediately began to channel Teddy himself and launched into an uncanny and very funny impersonation of the beloved Massachusetts senator. Suddenly from the other side of the crowded restaurant another Teddy impersonator jumped to his feet to loudly engage with Larson. It was then-Congressman Marty Meehan (D-MA) and we suddenly had Dueling Kennedys on our hands, with Boston accents, Kennedy mannerisms, and good-natured insults flying back and forth. This greatly amused my staff and about half of the restaurant's patrons and annoyed the hell out of the rest.

The point is if two politicians as different as Walter Jones and John Larson can come together to promote campaign reform legislation, then maybe there is some hope for the legislative process in Congress. If a conservative rural Republican and a liberal urban Democrat can find common ground on the need to get big money out of our campaigns, then the rest of us ought to be able to find the reform center to reclaim the dignity of our politics.

The progressive movement in America has led the charge since the days of Teddy Roosevelt for reform government and clean elections. We must continue the fight today. First and foremost, we must eliminate gerrymandering abuses when congressional districts are drawn. And we must fight for reform by championing government transparency, terminating no-bid contracts, and expanding public financing of elections.

Let's make it so our candidates in the future will be studying briefing papers or meeting voters at 9:30 A.M., instead of sitting down to a day of fund-raising phone calls.

CHAPTER SEVEN

No Little Plans

One day in 2011, in a meeting while I was serving as Montgomery County Commissioner, the county transportation planner Leo Bagley looked me in the eye and said, "We are a big county. We need big ideas to solve our big problems."

Leo Bagley is an outstanding public official and an expert on transportation issues, and I knew he was right. The problem we were facing was massive daily traffic jams on Route 422 in the western suburbs of Philadelphia, and a lack of federal or state funding to finance the necessary road improvements and new bridges that were needed to increase Route 422's capacity to handle all the cars during rush hour. The proposal he was advocating on behalf of the planners for the county and the Delaware Valley Regional Planning Commission (DVRPC) was to impose a local toll on drivers using Route 422 to raise money dedicated to fix the road, build the bridges, and extend commuter rail service to that area. It was a bold, exciting, and controversial plan.

I was chair of the DVRPC at the time, so it was my job to attend the public hearing called to discuss the commission's plan, and Leo wanted me to endorse the proposal to impose tolls and make local drivers pay to use the road on which they currently commuted for free.

I knew the tolling plan would be controversial, but I also knew the planners were right. The local tolling concept offered the quickest way to raise the necessary funds and would allow the region to control our own destiny by solving our own regional transportation crisis. We needed a big idea to solve this big problem.

Promoting big ideas to solve our challenges is nothing new in America. In fact, it is a hallmark of our national character and has been since the nation's founding.

"Make no little plans," said Daniel Hudson Burnham in 1893. "They have no magic to stir men's blood."[1]

Burnham was a leading American architect and urban planner in his day. He designed master plans for the development of a number of cities, including Chicago, Cleveland, Washington, D.C., San Francisco, and Manila. He also designed several famous buildings, including the Flatiron Building in New York City and Union Station in Washington, D.C.

Sometimes his timing was good but his luck was bad. His plans for the redesign of San Francisco were delivered to City Hall on April 17, 1906, the day before the 1906 earthquake. Now, that could have been an urban planner's dream—a destroyed city landscape with a fresh urban plan ready for implementation. But the city fathers moved hastily in other directions to rebuild the city, and the Burnham plans were ignored.

But Burnham was on to something. His was a call for broad vision, creativity, and boldness. He knew that the success of his plans, to say nothing of his future commissions and fees, depended upon stirring the public's imagination and capturing attention and support from public officials and private citizens alike.

But things don't always work out the way people plan. The public hearing on the DVRPC tolling proposal for Route 422 certainly met Burnham's objective to "stir men's blood." The angry crowd of 500 local residents booed and heckled throughout the presentation of the plan, and my remarks in support of tolling the highway were drowned out by angry shouts and catcalls. The other elected officials sharing the dais with me fell all over themselves to criticize the proposal and distance themselves from it, to the rapture of the audience. The tolling proposal went nowhere. Accordingly, the road remained unfixed, the bridges were not built, and the rail service was not extended. Of course, the massive daily rush hour traffic jams continued. Six years later, state transportation taxes were increased and construction to fix the rush hour mess on Route 422 finally started.

Progressives must not be afraid to offer bold, sensible, and balanced policies to "stir men's blood" and win public support. We must make the case to invest national resources in better public schools, new jobs, updated infrastructure, and stronger communities. We must create opportunity for all Americans.

The Chinese seem to understand this principle. They have a history of announcing huge governmental and cultural undertakings designed to improve China's circumstances, such as Mao's Great Leap Forward. Of course, the rigid political control of the Chinese Communist Party and its brutality toward its own people have caused many of these initiatives to fail and have hurt the very citizens the Chinese government says it wants to help.

But sometimes those big plans that China's central planners promote actually bring reform to the Chinese people and improve their lives. No Chinese leader was more successful in implementing big plans to bring economic and political reform to China than Deng Xiaoping, who served as deputy premier from 1978 to 1992 and was considered throughout that period to be the paramount leader in China.

Deng is best remembered in the West as the leader who opened China to foreign investment, global markets, and limited private competition. He signed historic accords with President Jimmy Carter in January 1979 that normalized diplomatic relations and reduced barriers to trade and investment.

Deng also deserves more recognition for the political reforms he brought to China, particularly the direct democratic elections he promoted when he assumed power in 1978 for the selection of village councils in the hundreds of thousands of rural villages across China. These local elections continue to this day and offer the 900 million rural residents of China some meaningful control over their local affairs. This sampling of local democracy offers the Chinese people both self-government at the local level and the blueprint for changing the strangling central control of the Chinese Communist Party at all other levels of government.

Of course, true democracy is strictly a local matter in China. While village committee elections are generally free with transparent administration, local nominations, and the use of secret ballot boxes, the Chinese Communist Party maintains rigid control of the election process for the "people's congresses" that are elected at the higher levels of municipal, county, provincial, and national government. Nevertheless, the political reforms started by Deng Xiaoping in 1978, and formalized by the National People's Congress in a 1998 "organic law of the villagers committees,"[2] have given the rural Chinese a democratic clout over their own local affairs and a taste of self-government that I hope is irreversible.

When Jimmy Carter signed those 1979 accords with Deng Xiaoping that normalized relations and encouraged trade, they also discussed the political reforms that Deng was starting in China. Deng told Carter that the political reforms were even more important than the economic reforms. President Carter described this to me during an extraordinary day that my wife Francesca and I spent with President and Mrs. Carter in Beijing, China, on September 3, 2001.

I had been invited to speak at an international symposium on village elections and rural society that was jointly sponsored by the Chinese Ministry of Civil Affairs and the Carter Center, which has worked to support the election process and foster better governance throughout China. President Carter was kind enough to include us in the full day of activities and meetings which he and Mrs. Carter conducted before and after the conference. The affection and respect of the Chinese for the former president was impressive. President Carter spoke passionately to us about his friendship with Deng Xiaoping, who had died in 1997, and his support for the political and economic reforms that Deng had championed in China. Both of the Carters seemed to feel that not enough attention had been paid to these accomplishments. Mrs. Carter in particular felt that her husband had not received the credit he deserved for his leadership in signing the 1979 agreements with Deng and assuming the political risks that came with forging closer ties with Communist China. I agreed with her then, and still do, as our economic ties and political engagements with China grow ever closer.

In 2001, the political reforms in China that we were celebrating only went so far. Although the accomplishments of Jimmy Carter may not have received enough attention, the Chinese government certainly paid a good deal of attention to Francesca and me during this trip. Our embassy cautioned us that our hotel room would surely be bugged and Chinese internal security forces would follow us. Sure enough, female Chinese agents routinely followed Francesca into the ladies room. They would burst into the stall as soon as Francesca vacated it and scour the joint, presumably to make sure she wasn't leaving behind any packages or stashing any information. It was a stark reminder of the power of the state and its distrust of the people.

In my remarks at the 2001 symposium, I congratulated the Chinese national government for establishing by law the system of democratic elections for village committees, but urged the government to provide for vigorous campaigning to allow candidates to communicate robustly with the people. I stressed that China must trust its own people, and when the Chinese government took to heart the principles of direct elections at all levels, the Chinese government would be as great as the Chinese people themselves.[3]

I hope that in the years to come China will continue to liberalize and will grow closer to us as friendly competitors. I believe this because the nearly one billion rural Chinese who now vote in village elections will inevitably demand more personal freedom and more economic opportunity from their national government. The Chinese Communist Party cannot possibly keep the lid on forever. The political and economic reforms started in the "big plans" of Deng Xiaoping will morph into the big plans of an entire nation: political freedom and economic opportunity for all.

Back home in America, the spirit and vision of Daniel H. Burnham is needed today more than ever in our public life. Many politicians, particularly on the conservative right, are embracing a pinched and limited view of the role of government at all levels to respond to our national challenges. They pander to the public unease over our economic future and offer hollow rhetoric and simplistic promises to cut taxes and shrink government as the cure-all for our slow economic recovery.

President Trump offers a different approach, willing to spend public money on needed investments such as public works and infrastructure projects. Donald Trump is a developer and a builder and he understands the benefits of big projects. Progressives should work cooperatively with the president to find common ground to improve our roads, bridges, water systems, and other public works.

We need to think big in the public square and embrace bold ideas. We must also act with fiscal responsibility, paying as we go in sustainable ways to implement our goals.

We must ultimately understand that the "little plans" of the conservative right are simply not going to solve our problems or improve the quality of our lives. Let's embrace, not deny, the necessary role of government to act both boldly and wisely to "stir men's blood" by creating opportunities for all.

The most immediate and important challenge facing the country is building our economic strength and creating jobs. While meaningful job creation comes from growth in the private sector, government spending and investment plays a vital role in spurring private markets and creating opportunities for businesses to grow and for people to improve their education, training, and job prospects.

We must focus on how to keep the jobs we have, create more, and train workers for jobs of the future. We need a comprehensive strategy to create jobs, build a strong workforce, help small business, and bring together our farms, suburbs, and cities as we move our economy forward.

The economy has changed and so must we. We can build a strong workforce through bolstered education and job training programs. We can help the private sector create high paying jobs through sound investments in clean energy projects and in the business sectors that have demonstrated that they will be the backbone of our 21st-century economy. We can use our public investments to revitalize our communities and pull people together. This is how we grow and maintain a robust economy in the future. This is how we will move the country to the progressive center by investing in people with prudent and fiscally responsible programs.

A Stronger Workforce: Investing in Education and Job Training

Everyone seems to agree that better education is the key to building better workforces for today and tomorrow. But there is a lot of disagreement on how to do it.

I am a strong supporter of public schools. My wife Francesca worked for 25 years as a public school nurse in Philadelphia, and our children Mary and Jake graduated from the local public schools in our suburban community. The concept of public education makes so much sense: everybody pays through their taxes for tuition-free public schools that accept all children and offer them all a good education. Our system of public education has offered a social and economic ladder upward for generations of Americans.

But public schools are not working well in many urban areas. Test scores are down, drop-out rates are up, and too many kids simply are not learning enough to succeed in a complex and competitive workplace. These schools need more resources, more parental involvement, and more accountability.

Conservatives relish blaming the teachers and their unions for the failings of public education. That is an incorrect and simplistic reaction to a complicated problem. But I agree that we cannot tolerate a system of education that puts the interests of adults ahead of the interests of the children. We cannot value job protection for teachers over their performance and effectiveness in the classroom.

Teachers, principals, and administrators must be held accountable, and those that excel at what they do should be paid accordingly, based upon their merit. Those teachers who have lost their zeal for teaching and their ability to connect with students, or who never had it in the first place, must be mentored and retrained. If that doesn't work, they must be removed from the classroom. We owe the students at least that much.

I don't mean to make this sound easy, because it isn't. Well-meaning and bipartisan efforts were launched, like President Bush's No Child Left Behind[4] and President Obama's Race to the Top,[5] which met with mixed results. Those initiatives had problems and drawbacks that needed attention, but they were good faith reforms that reinforced the nation's long-standing commitment to public schools.

We must learn from our failures and continue to encourage competition and best practices throughout public education.

No Public Dollars for Private Vouchers

There is a passionate interest in some educational circles for using public tax dollars for private schools, through vouchers or other payments. Most private schools are fine institutions and provide a terrific educational option for many families. In fact, my parents sent me to an independent private school where I received a wonderful education. But there simply isn't enough public money to go around. If we start to siphon off scarce tax dollars from the public system in order to support private and parochial schools, the public schools inevitably will suffer.

There is a limited pot of public money available at this point to support education. If we provide public vouchers for private schools, and if we expand funding to options such as public charter schools, there will simply be less money available for the traditional neighborhood public schools and the children who remain in them. Our highest obligation must be to provide a good public school for every child in America.

All of us can understand the frustrations that parents must feel if they believe that their child is stuck in a failing public school. If those parents cannot afford the tuition of the local parochial school or a nearby private school, it is no wonder that they would be delighted to receive a public voucher worth several thousand dollars from their local school board that the parents could use at any school of their choice, public or private, to secure a good education for their child.

Voucher proponents, including many from the non-public schools that would be in line to receive those government grants, speak in grand terms about the benefits of "school choice". But it is really the private institutions themselves who reap most of the benefits of school choice, as they remain free to accept or reject any prospective student with voucher in hand, while they continue to be free of many reporting requirements and public accountability for their performance as educators. It is bad public policy to establish a school financing system that allows public money to pass through the hands of parents to non-public schools that in turn are not accountable to the public.

Voucher proponents maintain that a healthy competition would be created by voucher-bearing students between the traditional public schools and all of the other school options that currently exist or might spring up with the prospect of public funding. But would this competition really benefit all students?

First, there is little credible evidence in the educational literature that vouchers actually have improved student academic performance. Voucher proponents often claim there is such evidence, but unbiased experts are

not convinced. The National Education Policy Center, a nonprofit education policy research center located in the School of Education at the University of Colorado, reviewed a number of reports and concluded there is
little reliable information about the competitive effects of vouchers.[6]

Second, what would a voucher-inspired school competition do for the
traditional neighborhood public schools from which students presumably
would be fleeing? It seems likely that the most troubled students would be
left behind, students challenged with unmotivated or neglectful parents,
behavior problems, learning and physical disabilities, language difficul-
ties, and trouble just learning. Those neighborhood schools would have
an even harder time educating the children that would remain behind
under a scheme of publicly funded private vouchers that reduced traditional public school funding, drained high-achieving students, and sapped
teacher and parental morale.

It is far better for us to focus our creativity, enthusiasm, and resources
on providing a good public school for every child in America.

A National Vision for Education

We need a national vision for education that goes beyond improving
the public schools and reserving public dollars for public schools alone.
We should change how we frame the issue: education is an investment
with a tremendous return for the country, and the best path is to invest
wisely for the long term by fully funding the programs that are proven to
work, not to trim education spending for short-term savings.

Let's target education spending toward specific goals aimed to maximize
student achievement, create the best possible learning environments for
children, and build and maintain a strong and successful staff of teachers
and education professionals. Let's use accurate metrics to promote more
effective student assessment, class sizes and instructional time, and support quality programs for teacher training, mentoring, evaluation and continuing development.

Early childhood and pre-K programs have been tremendously successful. Children entering kindergarten from early childhood programs
are well prepared. This benefits those children, and it benefits all children: a classroom of equally prepared children means a better, more
educational, more enriching experience for everyone. The cost savings
and benefits start immediately, but they continue for a lifetime: these
children have higher graduation rates, and they are more likely to go
to college and get better jobs. They are less likely to drop out of school,
engage in criminal activity, and rely upon the government's resources.

Similar investment in drop-out prevention and drop-out reengagement programs have demonstrated real success, offering a solid return-on-investment both for the taxpayers and the students who become high school graduates. We need to fund and encourage programs across the country that identify at-risk students and allow educators to provide curricular, logistical, and interpersonal support to keep those students on track for high school graduation, and we should support drop-out re-engagement centers, which provide resources to those who wish to return to school and complete their education.

We must set higher academic standards to improve the caliber of our education system. We owe our students a guarantee that a high school diploma is awarded for true achievement, and that the diploma signifies to employers a solid command of the knowledge and skills needed for success. Educators, advocates, and parents ought to be able to agree on the topics and the proficiencies children need to be learning and mastering.

We should use well-designed standardized tests, validated and calibrated by education researchers, to ensure that student achievement is accurately measured. Testing results will help measure how well the students are learning, how well the teachers are teaching, and how well the educational system is working.

As we raise standards and impose testing on those standards, we must also provide remedial and tutoring programs to help every student meet those standards. It makes no sense at all to raise academic standards and to devise thoughtful standardized testing to determine who is mastering those standards, if we don't also actually give extra attention to the students who are failing to measure up to those standards. The biggest failure of No Child Left Behind was that President George W. Bush never delivered the promised funding for the remedial programs that many students needed. Strong tutoring and other remedial supports are essential for good public schools.

Many teachers say they don't like "teaching to the test" and have become quite critical of standardized tests. Without a doubt, teachers are good people in an honorable profession doing a tough job that greatly benefits all of us. Good teachers are essential to our society's success and more of our finest young people should choose teaching as a career.

But the teachers miss the mark on this one. What is wrong with teaching kids to pass a test? In a massive public educational system, there must be measures in place to assure standards and achievement. Yes, No Child Left Behind has been underfunded, standardized tests need to be improved, excessive testing is wasteful, and we really want kids to be able to think critically, not just memorize and repeat facts. But there must be hard work and accountability both in teaching and learning. Teaching a kid what he or she needs to know to pass a test, and holding both teacher and student responsible if he or she doesn't pass, is common sense.

It is a sad indictment of the adults in our educational structure that when external pressure is applied through standardized testing to achieve results and impose accountability, some educators respond by corrupting the system and cheating on the testing procedure. Not everyone employed in public education today deserves to stay employed.

Every school needs a strong principal. This may be the most important reform of all. We need to enact whatever changes are necessary to collective bargaining agreements, school codes, administrative practices, and local customs in order to put the principal in charge of the school. A strong principal sets the tone for the entire school building and holds everybody accountable for doing his or her job, including teachers, students, parents, and staff. Further, a strong principal has everybody's back and protects the school community from unhealthy influences from inside and outside. No school will flourish in the presence of overbearing central administrators, irrational parents, bickering teachers, demoralized staff or bullying students. It is up to the principal to provide the leadership and crack the whip, and also to boost the morale and spur the creativity of everyone involved in the school. This is one of the many things I have learned from my wife Francesca through the years—in this case through her 25 years of experience as a school nurse under several principals in the Philadelphia public schools. When the principal is strong the school will flourish, and when the principal is weak the school goes to hell.

Finally, one of the best reforms we could enact to benefit public schools is to change the way we pay for education. Nationally, about 30 percent of public school funding is raised through local property taxes. Nobody like the real estate tax, since it is based on the amount of property you own, not on your income and your ability to pay. A local property tax makes some sense for financing local government, since there is a reasonable relationship between the size of your property and the amount of local services you need, such as police protection, road repair, and garbage collection. But there is no rational relationship between the size of your property and the local schools.

Good public schools are expensive. In the suburbs of Philadelphia, the schools consume about 80 percent of our local property tax revenue. This places a tough burden on retired homeowners, whose income has been reduced by retirement but whose tax burden remains to support public schools. To make matters worse, the unfair school property tax usually goes up every year. It is time to place the burden of financing public education less on property taxes and more on income and ability to pay.

Of course, higher education remains an essential ingredient in the recipe to improve our workforce. Every student must have the opportunity to continue their education through college, and scholarship programs at the state level are needed.

We must also increase access to community college programs designed to educate and retrain workers in the skills needed for 21st-century jobs. Those that stand to benefit the most from expanded community college opportunities are most likely to be out of work or underemployed. Increased funding and tuition assistance are necessary to bring these community-based programs within the economic reach of under-trained and unemployed workers who are anxious and willing to improve their skills and knowledge and thus boost their employment prospects.

Workers' Rights

A strong and healthy workforce is absolutely essential to support a strong economy. While job creation remains Job One, we also must ensure that the workers who take those jobs will be paid a reasonable income, be guaranteed fundamental rights, be covered by health and retirement programs that will protect them during and after their careers, and be treated equally.

Progressives support the federal minimum wage, both as an economic issue and as a moral imperative. A worker is entitled to a fair day's pay for a good day's work, and a worker should be guaranteed earnings sufficient to stay out of poverty. The federal minimum wage was set in July 2009 at $7.25 per hour, which provides a wage no higher after inflation than in the early 1980s. The federal minimum should be at least $5 an hour higher, which would merely restore the minimum wage to its historic high of about 50 percent of average wages. Further, such a boost would also restore the minimum wage to its broader function—helping to boost pay rates across the economy.

Conservatives always complain that such government mandates on business designed to protect and regulate working hours, wages, and workplace conditions simply drive up the costs of doing business and are counterproductive in a free market, capitalist economy. I see their point—there is no question that such mandates must be paid for and certainly increase the prices of the goods and services that businesses sell. But we decided as a society about 100 years ago that we are willing to pay the price for such worker protections as minimum wages, maximum hours, child labor restrictions, and workplace safety requirements. We are willing to pay more for what we buy in the free markets in order for workers to be treated fairly. The right wing needs to recognize this existing social compact and get used to it.

The right of labor to organize and bargain collectively is fundamental and has been settled law since the New Deal. Employers should not be allowed to intimidate workers in attempts to prevent unions from forming or to restrict or inhibit union activities. Progressives should support legislation to protect the rights of American workers to organize.

And while supporting the rights of workers, it is imperative that we also strive for those rights to be equal for all workers. Workplace discrimination related to employee wages, benefits, and rights must be ended. Employers should compensate workers for the value of their work—they should not be allowed to underpay for certain jobs that tend to be, or historically have been, disproportionately held by women.

One of the best tools to boost the economic status of working families is the refundable earned income tax credit currently in place at the national level and in several states and the District of Columbia. This tax break rewards work and is targeted at low-income workers and families.

One of the most critical roles government should fill in the job sector over the next few years is to help establish "career ladders" that will allow lower income workers to improve their skills and therefore their job prospects. Partnerships are needed between community colleges, unions, professional associations, and employers such as hospitals, casinos, and factories to allow entry level and low paid workers to advance. Such a career ladder, for example, could encourage very low paid home health aides to move up to become better paid nurses aides and then higher paid licensed practical nurses and registered nurses.

A stronger workforce requires better education, improved job training and expanded workers' rights. Progressive government embraces the need for public investments to accomplish those goals.

Investing in New Jobs and Clean Energy

We need more investment in our economy in order to create jobs and expand opportunity for all. During all the economic booms in our nation's history, most of that investment has come from the private sector. In good times, business leaders want to expand operations and find new markets, entrepreneurs want to start new businesses and are willing to take risks, and banks, pension funds, and other lenders are willing to provide the capital to allow these good things to happen.

But what do we do when times are not so good? We should not wait for the corporations that are hoarding their cash to decide to invest again. We should not wait for Wall Street leaders to develop social consciences and do something productive with their money other than grant big bonuses to each other. Waiting will take too long. Passivity is rarely a good strategy. Let's use our common resources to try to make some good things happen sooner rather than later.

Let's agree on a strategy for the prudent use of public dollars to supplement the private investment that our economy desperately needs. We must recognize that thoughtful, targeted public investments in economic development and community revitalization can reap bountiful returns in new jobs and new life for some of our most challenged communities and neighborhoods across the country.

We can start by seeking to attract, promote, and assist the industries of the future. We should adopt an "Invest Green in Green" strategy that will invest public dollars in the green economy. Opportunities abound in the fields of energy efficiency and conservation. Support for green energy will create jobs in manufacturing, construction and engineering. Development of alternative energy industries like wind, solar, geothermal, and biofuels will boost local economies. Workers need to be trained by state and local governments, community colleges, and nonprofits to fill these emerging jobs. A smart "Invest Green in Green" initiative will lead toward our national goal of energy independence, while creating new American jobs in the process.

In addition to encouraging our own private and public investments in alternative and renewable fuels and clean energy development, we need to attract foreign interest and investment from overseas companies that are industry leaders in alternative and renewable energy. Frankly, Western European companies are a generation ahead of our domestic energy industry in the profitable development of wind, solar, and other renewable fuels. We should do everything we can to attract foreign investment in the alternative energy industry in this country in order to create good paying jobs for Americans right now, while we catch up with the Europeans with our own commercial development of alternative energy. While the profits from these foreign investments will return overseas, nevertheless these companies will be employing Americans in their U.S. operations and will be paying our taxes.

States need to realize the role they must play in this competitive market if they want to attract foreign investment to create alternative energy jobs. When he took office as Pennsylvania's governor in 2003, Ed Rendell created World Trade PA,[7] the most energetic and well-funded effort by any state to encourage domestic exports and develop new overseas markets for Pennsylvania companies, while also competing for new direct investment by foreign companies into the state. Governor Rendell quickly realized that the biggest potential source of foreign investment would come from the big energy companies like Conergy in Germany and Gamesa in Spain that wanted to build their solar panels and wind turbines in America for the emerging American market. The Western European business leaders I met when I served as Pennsylvania's Deputy Secretary of International Business Development were anxious to expand their operations to our state because Governor Rendell was willing to invest state resources to develop the energy sector and attract these foreign investments. The strong, bipartisan support in the state legislature for attracting overseas investment was very important to the foreign business leaders weighing whether to invest in our state.

Citing the urgent need to cut energy costs, move toward energy independence, and stimulate the economy, Pennsylvania under Rendell's leadership dedicated $650 million in the Alternative Energy Investment Act to accelerate the state's leadership by significantly expanding investments in the alternative fuel, clean energy, and energy efficiency sectors, both foreign and domestic.[8]

Pennsylvania reaped the benefits of this aggressive strategy to commercially develop the alternative and clean energy industries. Thousands of jobs were created in the state as a result, and the state's unemployment rate during the Great Recession was consistently one or two percentage points below the national unemployment rate, which was not bad for a so-called rust belt state.

Now Pennsylvania has an unexpected economic opportunity with immense potential—the development of natural gas drilling in the vast Marcellus Shale formations that lie deep under the state. Recent technological improvements have made the recovery of natural gas in the state financially feasible. The rush is on to develop the industry quickly, pushed by the national energy companies anxious for new drilling areas and increased profits, and by the state government desperate for new revenue from royalties and leases, and by the property owners interested in lease payments for drilling and mineral rights on their land.

Natural gas drilling is creating jobs and wealth in Pennsylvania, without a doubt. But it also poses a real threat to the environment and to the quality of drinking water throughout the state. The gas drilling industry uses a process called hydraulic fracturing, or "fracking," to inject chemically treated water under high pressure to break up the shale deposits in order to release and capture the natural gas reservoirs.

The process of creating each natural gas well consumes over 2 million gallons of water drawn from local streams, rivers, and lakes. That water becomes contaminated in the drilling process by the abrasive chemicals added before the water is forced underground, and by the solids and minerals that the water scoops up underground during the fracking process. Then most of the wastewater returns to the surface and ultimately gets returned to our fresh water supply, becoming part of our ecosystem that provides drinking water to millions of people.

The industry must be required to clean up the water they use in the drilling process, before they put the water back where they first found it in our streams and lakes. The drilling wastewater is so contaminated by the chemicals added as part of the drilling operation and by the underground residue that standard sewage plants can't handle the steps necessary to clean up the water. We must ensure natural gas well wastewater is thoroughly processed by enacting and enforcing strong regulations at the state level, based upon the federal safe drinking water standards.

The solution to the revenue needs in Pennsylvania seems simple and straightforward—impose a reasonable and fair severance tax on the natural gas extracted from the ground, just as every other state does which has a significant natural gas industry.

Rigid Republican ideology that insists that any tax increase is always bad has prevented Pennsylvania from asking a successful industry to make fair tax payments for some of the costs imposed on the state. Instead, the taxpayers have to pick up the costs of regulating and inspecting the drilling operations and protecting the environment and safe drinking water supplies. This is right-wing corporate welfare at its worst, coddling a big, powerful industry and soaking the average taxpayer.

Most Pennsylvanians are looking for bipartisan consensus and political agreement to ask the natural gas industry to pay its fair share toward improving our infrastructure, protecting our environment, and promoting our economic development.

President Trump, to his credit, has championed new national investments in public infrastructure. Virtually every community in the country has a backlog of public works needs. Maintenance has been deferred on bridge, highway, water and sewer projects, and now new capacity must be created and expansions need to occur. We need a "Jobs Now" initiative at all levels of government to fast track infrastructure repair projects and pollution clean-up projects. Well-paying, family-sustaining jobs will result from investments in public works and green jobs. Smart investing will revitalize our communities and put people to work right now.

Growing Small Business

Clearly, small businesses are the heart of our economy and keeping them healthy is a top priority. About 90 percent of American businesses

are small businesses with fewer than 20 employees.[9] These are the companies that create most of the new jobs; but in a stagnant economy, these are
the businesses that are the hardest hit. They have fewer resources and less
money in the bank and less access to the financial capital that they need.
In today's economic climate where loans are difficult to come by, entrepreneurs find it harder to start new businesses.

We must expand health-care reforms that will provide small businesses
with more relief from the spiraling costs of health care. We must promote long-term capital loans and micro-loans to small businesses from
state governments, and additional federal support for the Small Business
Administration.

To better prepare the next generation of small business leaders, we must
explore incentives for small businesses to participate in university co-op
and internship programs. These partnerships will encourage technological
advances and business innovations we cannot even envision today.

Prudent but robust government action could make a huge difference
for the small business community. Congress should cut capital gains taxes
resulting from small business investments. Government guarantees should
be increased on small business loans, with lower fees and higher loan
limits. Tax credits for research and development, investments in plant and
technology, and new job creation should be more available for all businesses, large and small.

Government grants, loans, tax credits and deductions, and other public
subsidies are necessary and legitimate ways to create jobs and spur economic growth. We have to focus our public resources on economic sectors
with the most potential for growth and the greatest need for support.

Revitalizing Communities

Most states and regions of the country are comprised of urban, suburban, and rural areas, each with distinct challenges along with many shared
problems. Not surprisingly, most states and the federal government have a
myriad of programs to address those distinct challenges. The programs are
well meaning and certainly do more good than harm, but we need to do a
much better job responding to the needs of the communities where most
of us live. The challenge is not to devise more or even better programs.
The challenge is to plan better for our future and to better coordinate the
spending of public resources to help reach that future.

Most Americans live in cities large and small, in suburbs and on farms.
Lots of government spending is devoted to helping those distinct communities, but not enough is focused on how to develop connections between

those communities. Farms don't exist in total isolation from residential neighborhoods, and suburbs can't exist without the cities they surround. We need more connections, not more separations, and we need to consider how government spending, subsidies, and tax policies can be used to encourage the networks and regional connections we need.

Government infrastructure projects can strengthen those connections. For example, when we invest in public transportation, such as buses, trains, and trolleys, we create jobs in construction, maintenance, and transportation operations, as well as move people around a lot better. When we expand transportation and its infrastructure, we facilitate and support jobs throughout our cities and their surroundings through improved mobility, we improve the quality of life for families by cutting commuting times and getting breadwinners home sooner to their children, and we help the environment by reducing energy consumption and air pollution.

By investing in our roads, we not only increase highway capacity and reduce traffic congestion and gridlock but also, when done properly, encourage responsible development that will preserve both urban neighborhoods and suburban communities. Road and bridge repairs improve safety, create jobs, and quite literally keep us moving forward. With wise investments of transportation dollars to increase traffic capacity and personal mobility, coupled with transit-oriented design and zoning to guide new development, we can help our cities, suburbs, and rural communities work together as never before.

People are increasingly drawn to mixed-use developments that provide housing, offices, shops, and restaurants under one roof. This combination of "connections" and "community" has long been the major advantage of America's urban centers. We need a dynamic mix of development, public spaces, and public transportation to give our downtowns new life. Public investments to revitalize and rehabilitate older communities and downtowns will bring to many of our urban areas the economic growth and vitality that they haven't seen in years, in turn bringing renewed safety, prosperity, and pride.

Revitalizing our urban centers can provide the economic "pull" to complement the "push" of open space and farmland preservation programs, with a goal of protecting natural areas and attracting investment to areas already developed. We need to coordinate government spending to protect green fields, manage growth, and fight uncontrolled development and sprawl, while attracting private investment in downtowns and urban centers through government grants, loans, and tax breaks. It is cheaper for companies and developers to expand and build on farmland than to redevelop and rehabilitate in urban centers. But it is better for society for the private sector to invest and expand in developed areas with existing population density and public infrastructure already in place, while protecting our green assets so important to our quality of life. Government incentives can prime the pump and guide private investment where we want it and where it will do the most good.

If small business is the heart of our economy, creating most of the new jobs and nurturing most of the risk-taking, then the family farm is surely the soul of the economy, taking us back to our roots, while agriculture ranks as the leading industry in many states.

Small, family-owned farms are hurt by poor local planning, high property taxes, suburban sprawl, highway construction, and unregulated natural resource mining. Those farm families need our help.

If we can offer the huge agricultural corporations all manner of subsidies and tax breaks, then we better offer a hand to the family farmer as well. Let's make crop insurance more affordable, to help farmers reduce risk. Let's invest more in agricultural research, to increase crop yield. Let's improve support for marketing to encourage "buy local" campaigns and connect farmers and their consumers.

To help our small farmers in the marketplace, we need incentives for local, sustainable, and organic farms, which in turn will provide the customers of those farms with healthier diets.

We also need to bridge the widening divide between our farms and cities by bringing healthy foods to poor urban areas and encouraging community gardens. As modern farming requires increasingly specialized knowledge, children of farming families need greater access to educational opportunities than ever before, and the farmers need business advice to survive in the complex agricultural marketplace. Broadband Internet must be expanded throughout the country to give all of us, rural and urban, access to the online world.

We must expand open space preservation programs at the county and local level like the one I helped to start in suburban Montgomery County, Pennsylvania in 1993, as well as farmland preservation grants and tax breaks at the state level. Planning and spending on open space preservation, when done wisely and inclusively, has worked to bring communities together throughout the country and has successfully demonstrated the need for connections between city, suburb, and farm.

The Montgomery County open space program has preserved well over 10,000 acres of valuable land in our suburban community since its inception in 1993.[10] The wide public acceptance of the open space preservation program was due to good planning and lots of local involvement in creating the program. The county planning director, the legendary Art

Loeben, urged the county commissioners to create a preservation program to buy private real estate to protect valuable open space and fragile lands from suburban sprawl and to create new parks for both active recreation and passive enjoyment. Art included in his vision new recreational trails, protected stream banks and steep slopes, and preserved watersheds and "viewsheds." He stressed the need to involve local town governments and interested citizens in the crafting and implementation of the program. We appointed an Open Space Task Force to help write the plan, hold hearings, advise the commissioners and, very importantly, to help sell the final proposal to their fellow citizens.

The three county commissioners received the final report and recommendations from county staff and the citizens' task force, and with a bipartisan and unanimous vote started the county's open space program. It was the best thing we ever did.

Certainly, these strategies to revitalize communities must be "owned and operated" by citizens and local elected officials, even though considerable state and federal resources will be needed. Every community is unique, and we can't force a single government strategy to work everywhere. Many local organizations excel at providing job training, education, mentoring, housing, small business assistance, and neighborhood revitalization. We must empower and depend upon successful community-based organizations.

Another good example of rational planning, wise investment, and local involvement and control is the economic development program of Montgomery County that was launched in 2009.[11] We are a wealthy suburban county bordering Philadelphia with high per capita incomes, nice residential neighborhoods, busy shopping malls, and bustling office parks. But a number of our older communities and downtowns had fallen on hard times, with upscale shops relocating to those suburban malls with lots of parking and little new investment to modernize or renovate the urban centers left behind. So the county commissioners in 2008 decided to consider actions to attract private investments and to leverage government funding sources to revitalize our older towns.

We appointed a 35 member Economic Development Task Force comprised of local business leaders, community activists, labor leaders, and local elected officials. We hired an economic consulting firm for the task force and also assigned as staff our existing employees in the county planning and commerce departments. After six months of meetings, study and public hearings, the task force presented a comprehensive report to the county commissioners recommending the establishment of a county economic development plan, to include appointing an economic development director and pledging an investment of $105 million in county funds over seven years.[12] The report recommended eight specific initiatives:

1. Increased "seed" funding to expand existing community revitalization activities.
2. New "seed" funding for Main Street and downtown redevelopment in older boroughs and towns for projects focused on parking, rehabilitation of existing buildings, and upgrading retail corridors.
3. "Gap financing" for major redevelopment projects in the county's most economically challenged communities for large-scale, transformational, multi-building commercial, industrial, and residential developments.
4. Targeted business incentives for small businesses locating in the county's most economically challenged communities.
5. Support to develop the planning process and form the planning partnerships necessary to implement large-scale development initiatives undertaken within a framework of visionary and comprehensive strategic planning.
6. Reinvestment in and reuse of existing commercial space throughout the county, in particular in older office and industrial parks.
7. Targeting various incentives, marketing programs, and other initiatives to be carried out by local municipalities.
8. Targeting various workforce development programs, including contracting out job placement programs and expanding training programs available at the community college and other colleges and universities throughout the county.

In early 2009, the county commissioners considered the report at a public meeting and, after receiving numerous favorable comments from task force members and interested citizens, approved the report and authorized the economic development plan.

The Great Recession of 2008–2010 severely limited both the private and public funds that were available for economic development partnerships, but the county's program was successful immediately in creating and saving several hundred jobs in the county's urban centers. More important, the framework was now in place to boost our local and regional economy.

We have seen that there is an appropriate and even vital role for government at all levels to create a stronger workforce, invest in new jobs, and revitalize communities.

The private sector will create more jobs and will invest in more communities with appropriate public incentives. The government needs to educate and train workers, invest research and development dollars in growing sectors of the economy, and help connect our disparate communities.

Most important, we must do a much better job in coordinating the government spending that already exists. The projects funded by transportation dollars must also strengthen communities and help encourage smart growth. Economic development spending must attract and guide the all-important private investments to communities most in need of revitalization and jobs. Funding to protect green and open space must complement efforts to redevelop downtowns.

All of this spending is public money, and we need to spend it wisely and creatively if the taxpayers are going to allow us to keep spending it at all.

We can build a stronger workforce by investing in public schools and job training and by protecting workers' rights.

We can build our economy by investing in new jobs and clean energy. We can boost small business and revitalize our communities with coordinated programs of economic development, open space preservation, and transportation improvements.

We must think big and adopt no little plans, even during tough budgetary times, if we are going to win public support for our progressive policies and create new opportunities for all Americans.

CHAPTER EIGHT

Bring It Every Day

It was October 28, 2010, and Bill Clinton was campaigning in Norristown, Pennsylvania, for the Democratic candidate for governor, Dan Onorato. My friend Jim Maza was standing in the front row along the rope line listening to all the campaign speeches, and he was excited at the end of the program when the former president descended from the stage of the George Washington Carver Center and began to shake hands.

Jim Maza and I had been elected as Bill Clinton delegates from Montgomery County in the Pennsylvania primary in 1992 and voted to nominate Clinton for president that summer at the Democratic National Convention. We had to "commit" to the Clinton campaign by January of that year to be considered as delegates, which was considerably before the future president was well known in Pennsylvania. Jim and I have always been proud of our early support of Bill Clinton, and Jim was pleased to have a chance to speak with the former president on the rope line in Norristown.

Jim introduced himself to President Clinton, quickly mentioned his service as a Clinton delegate 18 years before, and thanked the former president for coming to town to support the Democratic ticket. Bill Clinton smiled, and then did a curious thing. He nodded his head back toward the stage he had just left and said, "How did I do?"[1]

Jim Maza told me later that he was very flattered by the question and began to give Clinton an earnest critique of the speech before he stopped himself and just laughed, thinking why in the world Bill Clinton, former president, world statesman, and international humanitarian, would give a damn what Jim Maza thought about his speech. Clinton just smiled again, nodded, and made his way down the rope line, thrilling other folks with a handshake or autograph or a kind word.

Jim and I agreed later that Bill Clinton probably did not care what Jim thought about the speech, but just as surely Jim had witnessed an in-grained technique that Clinton uses to connect with people. People are flattered when someone asks for their opinion, and when the asker is a former president of the United States then the compliment is high indeed. We figured that this habit of soliciting opinion from voters must come as naturally to Bill Clinton as shaking hands or kissing babies. We were duly impressed.

Bill Clinton was on a roll that October day. Following his appearance for Dan Onorato and local candidates in Norristown, he made a second stop in Montgomery County at Bryn Mawr College on behalf of Joe Sestak, the Democratic candidate for the U.S. Senate in Pennsylvania. I had left the Norristown rally early before Clinton spoke so I could get to Bryn Mawr and help warm up the crowd before the former president's arrival. After Clinton arrived at Bryn Mawr, I asked another friend, State Senator Daylin Leach, how Clinton had done in his earlier appearance in Norristown. Day-lin simply said to me with quiet admiration, "Bill Clinton always brings it."[2]

That's it. The secret to Bill Clinton's success is he always brings it. Here he is, a former president who makes millions every year on the lecture circuit and devotes enormous time and energy to humanitarian and peace-keeping work around the world, and he is still willing, and even eager, to hit the campaign trail every election cycle for state and local Democrats. He always brings enthusiasm and passion to every public appearance and every private meeting. He focuses like a laser on the crowd he is address-ing or the person he is talking to and he fully commits himself to that encounter and doesn't quit until he has given it his all. That is why he is always running late and his speeches are too long and he won't stop until he has shaken every hand in the room. He is always bringing it and that is why he connects so well with people.

Most Democratic politicians who were active in national politics in the 1990s have favorite Bill Clinton stories to tell to this day. The man seemed to be everywhere Democrats met and he dominated every gathering and appearance with his extraordinary ability to connect with people. He was both praised and mocked for his famous claim, "I feel your pain." The thing is, I really believe that he did feel people's pain. It was no act. The people sensed his sincerity and they loved him for it.

At least the Democrats loved him for it. Some of the Republicans through the years weren't so favorably inclined. They didn't like Clinton until they met him.

The best example of that in my experience occurred in late November 1998 following my first election to Congress. The new members-elect (Baby

Congressmen, my first chief of staff called us) were gathered in Washington, D.C. for orientation before being sworn into office in January. We were all invited one evening, Democrats and Republicans alike, to visit the President and the First Lady in the White House. On the way over in the chartered bus from our hotel to the White House, I overheard some tough talk and bravado among my new Republican colleagues about Bill Clinton. They were muttering about his shortcomings and failures and wondering aloud how he proved to be so resilient and whether he would survive the impeachment proceedings currently underway, and they were promising each other not to be taken in by his sweet talk and Slick Willie persona.

My new Democratic colleagues and I started nudging each other and sharing amused glances. We realized that none of the Republican first-termers had ever met Clinton before or been in his presence or been subjected to the power of his personality. All they had learned about Bill Clinton had come from the angry, nasty critics of the Vast Right Wing Conspiracy that Hillary accurately identified. After six years of his presidency, all of the new Democrats were personally familiar with the president and his magnetic personality. We were looking forward to the show.

Sure enough, Bill Clinton was dazzling that night. He greeted us all warmly and by name, even the Republicans, and shared a few words with each of us demonstrating his knowledge of our careers and our districts. He acted as the tour guide-in-chief, taking us all around the White House. He took us to his private study on the second floor where the family quarters are located, and identified every item, trinket, and memento on his desk, on the tabletops or hanging from the walls and where he got it or who gave it to him. He took us onto the Truman Balcony off the study to show us the sights. He gave us free access to the guest quarters, and provided an open bar, to boot.

Personally, my favorites were the Truman Balcony, where I got goose bumps, and the Lincoln Bedroom, where I sat and bounced on the bed a couple of times.

The real fun was on the bus on the way back to the hotel. The Republicans were awestruck. They couldn't believe what they had just experienced. Simply put, they were charmed by Bill Clinton and impressed by the trappings of the White House. They were sharing their amazement with each other with such childlike wonder that we Democrats started mocking and heckling them. Pretty soon the bus was rocking with good-natured insults and bipartisan laughter that really broke the ice among all the newbies. The good memories of Clinton Night stayed with the members-elect of the 106th Congress for quite some time.

Clinton stories abound. I recall an outdoor campaign rally one evening in the spring of 2008 at North Penn High School in Montgomery County when Hillary Clinton was running for president in the Pennsylvania primary. Bill Clinton was the headliner for his wife, who was campaigning elsewhere, and he drew a nice crowd of several thousand people. When he worked the rope line after the speech, an amazing number of people thrust things into his hands for his signature, such as books, photos, mementos, or just pieces of scrap paper. I was used to watching big time politicians hastily scribble their signature on items, while they steadily moved down a rope line, but Bill Clinton was different. He handed every item thrust at him to an aide walking behind him, who in turn would urge the supporter to wait there for the item to be returned. Then, after he shook every hand and posed for every picture, Clinton went inside to the lobby, sat down at a table piled high with all the objects, and carefully signed each one with a personal greeting, and an aide returned the signed memento to the supporter waiting outside. I could not believe the care he was taking to please each one of his wife's supporters, which must have added 30 minutes to his visit. When I expressed my amazement, Bill Clinton looked at me and just said, "I want her to win."[3] And Hillary Clinton did win the Pennsylvania primary in 2008.

The longest period of time I spent alone with President Clinton was during a ride in the presidential limousine in the fall of 2000 from Philadelphia International Airport to Independence Hall in Philadelphia, where the president was scheduled to sign a bill into law promoting the use of technology. I remember three things about that ride. First, how the president of the United States checked himself out in a mirror in the back seat of the limo and then licked his fingers and slicked down an unruly tuft of hair. Second, his extraordinary knowledge of the congressional districts in southeastern Pennsylvania and southern New Jersey as he quizzed me about the political lay of the land. Finally, most of all, his uncanny sense of timing in knowing when to turn away from our conversation in the back seat to the side window just as the limo was passing pedestrians on the streets of Philadelphia. The bystanders were in my line of sight, and just as they were taking notice of the presidential motorcade passing by and beginning to turn to gawk at the big black limo in the middle, Clinton would turn away from me in mid-sentence, make eye contact with the surprised citizens and give them a little wave. The looks of astonishment and joy on their faces were a sight to see. Clinton's hand would drop and he would turn back to me with hardly a break in the flow of the conversation, only to repeat the process at the next corner. He was just months away from leaving office and Bill Clinton was still connecting with folks.

He was still bringing it in 2016. On Primary Night in New Hampshire, after Hillary lost the primary to Bernie Sanders, I watched from the gym floor as Bill climbed into the bleachers to chat with supporters, lingering there after Hillary had finished working the rope line after her speech. She and the Secret Service had to wait for him to climb down and join them. And the crowd loved it.

Of course, many presidents have connected very well with the American people. Ronald Reagan obviously is a great example. His sunny optimism, avuncular style, and "Morning in America" approach to politics and governing made him extraordinarily popular. People trusted Ronald Reagan and knew he was sincere in his passionate advocacy of conservative values. When he made a mistake or a policy decision went awry the public was forgiving, believing it to be an honest mistake by a kind soul with a good heart. His "Shining City on a Hill" metaphor for the country,[4] with its biblical roots and upbeat vision, made people happy and proud to be Americans.

Other presidents, not so much. While Bill Clinton was feeling our pain in his televised debate with President George H. W. Bush in 1992, the first President Bush was caught on TV glancing at his watch and giving the impression he wanted to get the hell out of there.[5] No surprise that Clinton won the debate and, subsequently, the presidency.

President George W. Bush presents an interesting study. After his close and contested victory over Al Gore in 2000, due to the enthusiastic aid and active intervention of the conservative wing of the United States Supreme Court, George Bush hit the ground running with his tax cuts and conservative agenda and found himself with approval ratings of about 50 percent in early September 2001. Then, after the horror of 9/11 and the outpouring of patriotic emotion, President Bush's approval ratings soared to 90 percent. But those ratings didn't stay there and steadily dropped during the two Bush terms until he left office with approval ratings in the mid-thirties. George W. Bush was not able to sustain that connection with the people that is necessary for lasting popularity.

Donald Trump has started his presidency with historically low poll numbers. He got off to a very rocky start with spurious claims that exaggerated the size of his inaugural crowds and falsely alleged massive voter fraud that he blamed for costing him the popular vote majority. The new president made no effort in his inaugural address to reach out to his critics or unify the country. But he also has followed through on many of his campaign promises with a flurry of executive orders and legislative proposals that are very popular with his base voters. In the early months of his presidency, most Americans clearly either love or hate Donald Trump.

Progressives must understand why some presidents connect better with the public and stay more popular than other presidents. More to the point, progressives must make sure that *we* connect better with the public and stay more popular than our friends on the right wing.

We have to bring it. Find that passion within ourselves for the important work we are doing in the public marketplace. Communicate our ideas and our sincerity without hesitation or embarrassment. Let people see our emotion and our commitment to our principles and to public service. Connect with people by demonstrating through word and deed that we get it, that we understand the challenges that people are going through. We have to bring it every day, and that is the only way we will find and hold the progressive center in American politics and government.

We need a progressive farm team of future candidates, writers, bloggers, and opinion shapers. We have to teach and train this farm team how to bring it in progressive politics and public advocacy so we motivate the voters to follow us and move together to the progressive center.

Sometimes in politics the simple things are the most important. If you want to win someone's vote or influence his or her opinion, you have to first form a bond. There has to be a certain level of trust and good feeling before anything good can happen in politics. I spent 40 years in public life trying to get people to give me their support, their votes, and their money. There are two ways to do it: connect the dots and speak from the heart.

Connect the Dots

If the people of the country are going to give their votes to progressives, trust us with political power, and follow our leadership to the progressive center, we have to be able to connect with them first. We have to persuasively communicate our ideas and policies, effectively present our personalities and abilities, and win the confidence of the voters.

In short, we have to be good candidates, or at least better candidates than our worthy opponents.

Speaker Tip O'Neill's famous advice was all politics is local,[6] and he was correct. Every political exchange between vote seeker and voter is based on the local and personal needs of that voter and his or her perception about how well the vote seeker understands those needs.

I believe it all starts with the handshake. The fundamental political exchange is the handshake, the moment when the candidate presses the flesh and grasps the voter's hand in his own and communicates to the voter through that physical contact that the candidate understands the voter and can solve the voter's challenges.

A poor handshake can be a killer. A limp, half-hearted dead-fish handshake will tell the recipient he is not important enough to warrant a firm clasp of hands.

There may be deep psychological reasons why good political candidates instinctively stick out their hands to press the flesh with every voter. At a political workshop years ago, a speaker got a big laugh by accusing all of us assembled candidates of continually shaking hands in a desperate attempt to see if the average man on the street was still willing to touch us. Perhaps the act of handshaking is as simple as that—a reassurance of our common humanity.

In 1973, I was a low level staffer in the congressional office of Gerry Studds (D-MA). In preparation for his reelection, Congressman Studds sponsored a fund-raiser one evening at a private venue on Capitol Hill and most of the staff voluntarily attended. The special guest was Speaker of the House Carl Albert. It was an honor for the Speaker to attend the first fund-raiser in Washington, D.C., for a first-term member of the House. When the Speaker arrived, we staffers eagerly lined up to greet him, all excited to meet the great man. Imagine our disappointment when Speaker Albert quickly worked his way down the line of staffers, offering a dead-fish handshake, not making eye contact with anybody, mumbling blandly, "Nice to meet you. Nice to meet you." I remember that the Speaker looked me squarely in the stomach as he mumbled "Nice to meet you."

Now, Carl Albert certainly was a successful politician. Nobody rises to the Speakership of the U.S. House of Representatives without being truly gifted in the art of politics. The problem was he apparently wasn't willing to share those gifts with lowly congressional staffers.

You have to be able to deliver a firm, hearty handshake to a stranger, and look him squarely in the eye, if you hope to turn him into a friend.

How many times in a social setting have you shaken hands with someone who is not looking you in the eye? Maybe they are glancing over your shoulder trying to remember the name of the person next to you, or maybe they are counting the number of people in the room. It doesn't matter why they are not making eye contact with you, what matters is the impression they are giving to you—which is you are not the most important person in the room. That makes a very bad first impression. So look them in the eye.

And don't mumble to people "Nice to meet you" as Carl Albert did. First of all, don't mumble. Second, don't tell them it is nice to meet them.

Maybe you already met them and they will be offended that you don't remember. Don't tell them it is nice to see them again. Maybe you never met them and they will peg you for a phony. Just tell them it is nice to see them. And when you say it, mean it. They will be able to tell the difference.

But promoting ourselves and selling our progressive ideas requires more than just making a good first impression. We also need to win support in campaigns and in the public arena of ideas and debate. That requires getting the broad attention of the electorate, touching the voters on a personal basis, and persuading them we can be trusted with public office.

It always helps raise the visibility and credibility of a first-time or little known candidate to make appearances with and win endorsements from better-known politicians or celebrities. The finest example of the power of celebrity in my career was a memorable day I spent with "Lou Grant" during my 1984 campaign for Congress.

Ed Asner had played the television role of Lou Grant in two very popular series, "The Mary Tyler Moore Show" from 1970 to 1977 and "Lou Grant" from 1977 to 1982. By the time the Democratic Congressional Campaign Committee secured his appearance for me in 1984, Asner's shows had been off the air for two years. But you never would have known it.

Ed Asner was recognized and greeted warmly by virtually everyone we saw during that crowded campaign day. His face recognition was almost universal, not just at the press conference, television interview, and fund-raiser we scheduled, but also at the Plymouth Meeting Mall and walking down Main Street in Manayunk, a Philadelphia neighborhood. Absolutely everyone seemed to know who he was.

Now, his admirers did not always get his name right. A number of people shouted out, "Hey, Lou!" and "How's Mary?" But they all knew who Ed Asner was. This was my first experience with the awesome influence of television, and the almost frightening power of celebrity.

Happily, Ed Asner is a wonderful man who cheerfully and generously used his celebrity status to pull thousands of people into the Hoeffel for Congress campaign that day in 1984. His friendliness and sincerity was obvious to all. He connected with the people in a very warm and real way. It wasn't his fault that I got thumped in the election that fall.

Campaigning with big shots is a tried and true method in American politics. It is a great way to gain attention, establish credibility, and raise money. But the celebrity visits are few and far between in most campaigns. Most of the time, candidates simply have to go out themselves, or with a small group of helpers, and press the flesh and ask for votes.

The importance of meeting voters face to face cannot be overstated. There is no better way to win a vote than to look a voter in the eye and ask for his support. When running in large districts, congressional campaigns or statewide contests, the most enthusiastic campaigner can only meet a very small percentage of the potential voters. But in local elections with small budgets, vigorous retail campaigning with lots of voter contact and handshaking is absolutely essential.

I have knocked on tens of thousands of doors in my career, and surely have shaken hands hundreds of thousands of times with unsuspecting citizens who were minding their own business at supermarkets, commuter train stations, shopping centers, and neighborhood events. I always enjoyed this one-on-one campaigning. But the craziest version of retail politics I ever experienced was touring bus stops in West Philadelphia with Al Spivey.

Al was a smart, industrious political operative with a lifetime of involvement in Philadelphia politics and government. In 1984, he was part of the political organization of State Representative Chaka Fattah, my friend and colleague then in the State House and later in Congress. Chaka offered me his political team in West Philadelphia, where I was unknown, for my congressional election.

Al Spivey would drive down Haverford Avenue, the major road in the neighborhood, during the morning rush. Al would quickly pull over at bus stops where passengers were gathering to catch the bus that was usually only a block behind us. Al would push me out of the passenger door as the car screeched to a stop, yelling at me to start shaking hands with the waiting crowd. I would hurriedly shake every hand in sight, while Al would jump out of the car and thrust a brochure into those same hands. Then we would pile back into the car and peel out of the bus stop lane, usually when the bus was pulling in right behind us. We were off to the next bus stop a block or two away, often jumping the lights to make sure we stayed far enough ahead of the bus to have time to shake hands. We stayed one block ahead of the bus until its route downtown crossed out of the boundary of the congressional district in which I was running, and then we would double back and start the process again with the next bus. Al swore this was how they did things in West Philadelphia politics. It was so harrowing for me that I only did it once, but I will never forget my experience with the most intense retail campaigning of my life. I have no idea what those startled passengers must have thought when this frantic candidate leaped from a car, hastily shook their hand, then tore off, all while they were quietly lining up to get on the bus on their way to work. Al guaranteed me that we were doing more good than harm. I hope he was right.

In reality, pressing the flesh and face-to-face campaigning is simply not adequate in larger campaigns to make a major difference, because there are too many voters to meet. If progressives are going to connect the dots with people and convince them of the soundness of our ideas on a large scale, we also need to connect with them through the media. We have seen the wisdom of Tip's Advice about all politics being local, so let me suggest Tip's Corollary: the best politics is the most personal.

The best political connection through any kind of media is the most personal contact you can manage with your target audience. It doesn't matter if the media is traditional, electronic, or social. If you want to win a vote, lobby a public official, persuade a reporter, or influence an opinion maker, the best contact will be the most personal.

So, in traditional methods, a face-to-face meeting with your target is better than a phone call, which is better in turn than a handwritten letter, which is better than a typed letter, which is better than a signed petition. The more personal the contact made by the candidate/lobbyist/petitioner, and the more strenuous the effort to make the contact, the more influential the appeal will be. Voters are very impressed when candidates personally call them on the phone. But they are more impressed when candidates take the time and make the effort to knock on their door. Particularly if it is a hot summer day and you are sweating all over your clipboard and brochures.

Modern electronics and technology have created all new ways to greet voters and make your pitch. Some of them surely have been overused and have lost their effectiveness. For example, nobody should rely anymore on automated telephone calls, or robocalls, to do much positive persuading. Most people are sick and tired of receiving them. It is so impersonal for a local candidate to send a recording through the telephone, which is after all such a personal medium. Robocalls are okay to remind people what hours the polls are open or when a public meeting is scheduled, but as a method of persuasion they probably do more harm than good.

E-mail is better. It is easy to dash off a request or a message via e-mail. But it is also easy to send a hasty or flip reply, and even easier to ignore or brush off the contents of a serious e-mail chain. I believe e-mail campaigns have lost some of their impact. It remains a great way to let a lot of people quickly know about a meeting or a pending bill, but it is not a good way to persuade somebody of actually doing something. An e-mail in your electronic inbox is easily ignored, while a personal letter on your desk is not.

Facebook, Twitter, and other social media have proven to be very effective in communicating emotional messages to large numbers of people. Donald Trump through frequent use of his Twitter account certainly has demonstrated the ability to rally his troops with glib promises, vague claims, and personal insults directed at his critics. Trump has also shown a mastery of the art of public relations by using his simplistic tweets to distract the media and the public for a day or two from other major news stories that are unflattering to his presidency. Progressives must also master the use of social media to promote our message and rebut our opponents, hopefully in a way that brings people together rather than divides or demonizes them.

Television advertising is the best example of Tip's Corollary that the best politics is the most personal. No other form of advertising comes close to the TV ad's power to connect with voters, not billboards or mailings or handouts or bumper stickers. The reason is clear—the TV ad reaches and moves the viewer on an instinctive and personal level. TV ads can make you laugh, make you cry, make you angry, or make you happy. Lately, the consultants seem mostly to be aiming for anger. But the point is that TV ads move people in emotional ways, and that is the heart of personal persuasion.

Politics is tough. The best person does not always win. If you are running for office, I hope you have enough money to go on television with an adequate ad buy. If you don't have enough money, I hope your election district is small enough for you to reach most of the voters through door knocking and other personal politicking. If the district is big, I hope one party dominates your district and you are the majority party candidate. If none of those things is true, you are in for the challenge of your life.

So learn how to shake hands. Learn how to communicate honestly and personally with the voters. Connect with them on as personal a level as you possibly can. If they don't think you care, if they don't think you are listening to them, then they won't follow you anywhere.

Speak from the Heart

A good, persuasive speech is a thing of beauty. It is a rare work of art. In politics, it is much attempted and seldom achieved.

But progressives must learn to communicate effectively and touch people both in their minds and their hearts if we are going to win popular support and move people to the progressive center of American politics. After a lifetime of making speeches, most of them mediocre, I have learned some lessons and picked up a few tips.

A good speech rarely occurs when the speaker reads from a written text. Such a speech seldom flows naturally and often has too little eye contact between the speaker and the audience. It doesn't generate the natural connection between people that is needed in order to persuade or motivate an audience. A speech, after all, is supposed to involve speaking, not reading.

Modern technology has brought the teleprompter to the speechmaker's craft. It allows the speaker to seem to be making eye contact with the audience, while actually reading the text that is projected onto small glass panels on each side of the podium, or onto a panel on the front of the camera where the speaker is looking. The teleprompter helps keep the speaker's nerves at bay by removing the need for memorization and also eliminates the awkward shuffling of papers of a printed speech text. It keeps the speaker on point and on time throughout his delivery.

But the teleprompter also has its drawbacks. After all, the speaker is still *reading* the speech, which means it is still a challenge to avoid the unnatural pauses and hesitant cadences of reading from a written text.

The occasional use of a teleprompter is fraught with danger for a public speaker that is not used to the procedure and technique. The national Democratic Party recognizes this and provides training and tips on speaking to the national conventions where the use of teleprompters is mandatory. Their main expert consultant is the talented Michael Sheehan who has made a successful career of teaching the art of communication.

The challenges of a live speech to a televised national convention using a teleprompter were well documented in the "tip sheet" that Michael Sheehan[7] handed out to all convention speakers at the Democratic conventions where I have spoken. His admonitions include don't forget to smile, don't shout, don't grasp the lectern with a "death grip," don't be affected by applause or talk in the hall, deliver the speech with slightly more emphasis, slightly less speed and just the same volume as normal speaking style, don't ad lib or go off text, and don't wear clothing with patterns. That is great advice, but it is a lot to remember for a nervous convention speaker.

Sheehan particularly warns speakers of the dangers of simply swiveling or jerking their heads from prompter screen to prompter screen as they read the text. At the national conventions, there are four teleprompter screens, one on each side of the podium, one down in the podium, and one large one straight ahead across the hall. Sheehan points out that it looks far more effective and natural both to the audience in the hall and the TV audience at home for a speaker to turn slightly toward the side screens by moving shoulders and upper torso together rather than just moving the head. He urges a speaker while turning to always keep the microphone between you and where you are looking and to have short stretches of eye contact on one screen followed by saying a few words while looking off screen, while turning to pick up the speech text on the next screen. Simply put, Sheehan wants the speakers to look natural.

This was almost more than I could handle in 1996 when I was scheduled to speak to the Democratic convention in Chicago. I was a nervous wreck as the day of my first nationally televised speech approached, even though I knew that as a congressional challenger to a Republican incumbent my speech would be relegated to the middle of the afternoon when the TV audience is small.

I had lunch that day with my wife Francesca, and I was bemoaning all the things I had to remember and all the Michael Sheehan tips I had to internalize, particularly his warning against any unnatural jerking of my head from one prompter screen to another. After listening for awhile to my worries and nervousness, Francesca looked at me calmly and said, "Honey, relax. I have the answer. All you have to do is stare straight ahead at the big screen across the hall while you are speaking, and don't take your eyes off it. Then, just keep swiveling your shoulders from side to side as you talk." That image, and her demonstration of it at the lunch table, got me laughing so hard that it swept away my nerves and I got through the speech later that afternoon with no major blunders.

The best single piece of advice I ever received from Michael Sheehan was not from his convention speech "tip sheet" but from a candidate training session he ran for several congressional candidates back in the 1980s, courtesy of the Democratic Congressional Campaign Committee. As part of his media training, Sheehan urged us to be very careful about our facial expressions and head nodding during television interviews. Since the candidate might be on camera even when the interviewer is asking the question, it is damaging if the candidate is unconsciously nodding his or her head up and down during hostile or challenging questions. Sometimes candidates will affirmatively nod just to indicate they are hearing the question or to encourage the questioner to hurry up and finish so the candidate can give the answer, but the head nod gives the impression of agreeing with the substance of the question. Sheehan counseled us to always slightly nod in agreement and smile during friendly questions and sadly shake our heads from side to side and frown during hostile questions. He is completely correct—it is amazing how often I see candidates and public figures on television sending the wrong facial and head signals during interviews.

One of the habits of President Obama early in his presidency that really surprised me was his heavy reliance on teleprompters during many of his speeches and press events. Barack Obama is one of the finest public speakers I have ever seen. In fact, his extraordinary ability to motivate people through the spoken word is a major reason his 2008 campaign for president was so successful. Accordingly, it was almost shocking to see his frequent use of the teleprompter once he became president even for the most routine of his public speeches and announcements. Obviously, he was determined to get every word right and say just exactly what he wanted to say, but his remarks lost their spontaneity and power to persuade. Happily, he later restricted use of the teleprompter to major efforts like the State of the Union address.

Most of us rarely if ever use a teleprompter, but we still need to be able to deliver a speech that is interesting and persuasive, whether with prepared remarks or off the cuff. If we can't do that we will have little impact in the contest of ideas and policy in the public square.

There is nothing wrong with using notes or an outline while making a speech. Political staffers always call these "talking points." They contain your major points and are very useful during the speech to keep you on track and on message. These notes also give you a sense of security as you are speaking that you won't freeze and totally forget what you want to say. The key is to spend more time during the speech making eye contact with the audience than looking at your notes.

Winston Churchill, whose speeches in 1940 literally rallied his nation and the entire free world, wrote out his speeches word for word and then memorized them. He obviously understood the importance of making eye contact and connecting with his audiences, and he trained himself to deliver a memorized speech in a natural way with normal speaking cadences. But he liked to hold the speech transcript in his hands as he spoke because it gave him confidence and he could easily refresh his memory if necessary.[8]

There are several well-worn templates for how to make a good speech. They include "There are only two things you need for a good speech, content and delivery" as well as "Tell them what you're going to tell them, tell them, then tell them what you told them." Those old chestnuts are all well and good but are not very helpful to a novice or nervous public speaker.

Over the years, I have focused on four rules of speechmaking:

1.   Open with words that unite you with your audience.
2.   State clearly the purpose of your remarks.
3.   Present your main point as early, as often, and as directly as possible.
4.   Close with a reference to a higher ideal.

Another way of saying that is the speaker should shake hands with the audience, state his business, present his sound bite, and then take them to the mountaintop.

It is all about connecting with the audience, making them feel you understand and care about them, and then delivering a forceful, well-structured argument that uses repetition and emphasis to persuade them and win them over to your side.

The best speech coach I ever had was the late Dr. Robert Haakenson, Dean of Speech and Communication at Temple University in Philadelphia and one of the greatest all-time Democrats in the history of Montgomery County, Pennsylvania. My files contain several sheets of my handwritten notes compiled through the years summarizing Haakenson critiques after Bob had suffered through another one of my imperfect speeches. My notes contain such timeless good advice as make eye contact to open in command, offer warm greetings and salutations to put people at ease, use humor, use specifics, use pauses and avoid "I think."

Particularly good Haakenson advice is that the speaker must "think the thought" with evident commitment to the message being delivered. Otherwise the audience may conclude the speaker is merely posturing and pandering, which is a bad way to try to motivate people.

One of my cherished notes is actually in Bob's handwriting and contains five basic principles for good speechmaking that he dashed off for me one night in about 18 seconds. I reproduce it here verbatim:

1. Pause/smile/count the house

2. Schmooze with specifics, upbeat, humor

3. Preview three critical issues most appropriate to group

4. Develop those issues briefly, with immediate audience's perspective

5. Hard hitting, crisp recap, and haymaker to close. Terminal pause, holding eye contact. Avoid "thank you."

There it is, everything you need to know about making a good speech. You could spend a lot of money on books, classes, and training sessions and not learn anything better or wiser about the art of using the spoken word to influence people.

The most unusual advice in Bob's five basics is the admonition not to end a speech with "thank you." Bob believed that speakers reflexively use "thank you" at the end of speeches in order to avoid rambling as they think of all the things they forgot to say, or to make themselves shut up, or to signal to the audience that the speech is over and it is time to applaud. Bob maintained that a well-organized and crisply delivered speech virtually ends itself, and the speaker shows more confidence and is more persuasive by maintaining eye contact through the terminal pause and then walking away from the podium.

To this day I end every speech with "thank you." It is a thoroughly engrained habit that I cannot break. I don't have the nerve to follow Bob's advice and he would be disappointed.

But I have corrected a really bad habit during my speeches that caused Bob great professional pain. I used to punctuate my main points with a gesture that involved pushing my right hand toward the audience with palm forward and fingers curled. Bob described the move as a predatory spread of fingers and dubbed it "The Claw". Bob hated The Claw because of its negative impact on an audience and worked me over until I broke myself of that bad habit.

On March 12, 2003, I had the sad duty and high honor of speaking at Bob Haakenson's funeral. I did my best to repay Bob that day by remembering his sound advice as I spoke about his wonderful life. Of course, I told the story of his valiant efforts to deliver me from the clutches of The Claw, and as I demonstrated the hand gesture many of his old friends in the crowded church smiled and started doing The Claw back at me. It was a great moment. But I slipped up and ended those remarks with "thank you."

So this is what progressives have to do if we want to gain and hold the trust of the people. We have to think and speak with clarity, conviction, and vision. We have to tell the truth, connect the dots, and speak from the heart.

We have to bring it. We have to bring it every day. We have to believe in our good ideas and ourselves. We have to convince and motivate the public to join us in finding and holding the progressive center.

Conclusion

Unless he mends his ways, Donald Trump will fail as president of the United States.

Granted, President Trump and his family probably will leave office far wealthier than when he took office. The Trump coffers will swell because of his refusal to divest from his company to prevent undue enrichment and to avoid ethical conflicts with his public duties as president.

But without some changes, President Trump will fail as our national political leader. He is too negative and too egotistical. He makes untrue or wildly exaggerated statements. Americans want presidents to focus on us, but our new president focuses too much on himself.

He does not seek to unite the country but prefers to divide and demonize his critics. He is not growing his political base. He is not reaching out to the majority of voters who cast their votes for someone else. He is not trying to win over his opponents or even those who are unsure about him.

I take no pleasure in this prediction. I want my president and my country to succeed. We all need our president and our country to succeed. I see tough times ahead for our nation under President Trump, and that is not a good thing for any of us. Our country needs to thrive in a challenging and dangerous world.

Americans want cheerful, optimistic, and inspiring political leaders who make us feel good about ourselves, our country, and our future. We want a happy warrior as president, like Ronald Reagan or Bill Clinton. President Trump needs to fill that role.

Donald Trump had the rockiest first month in office of any president in our history, with the possible exception of William Henry Harrison, who died 31 days after taking office in 1841. But Trump is a smart man and a master of public relations and self-promotion. He will work hard to keep his campaign promises, which will please his base of supporters.

The progressive community must step forward and offer a positive plan for America to succeed in the Age of Trump. The fight for the progressive center in our politics will not be easy, and we must be prepared for abuse and opposition from the president's loyal base of supporters.

We must learn to tell our story. We must communicate our proposals and our values in a way that means something to the average American, particularly in the working class. We must put our story forward to compete with the dark vision of the Age of Trump, and we must persist until we win.

Most politicians learn at an early age about the power of stories, the power of a good narrative, to connect emotionally with an audience. Good stories that are well told are extremely helpful in the public contest for votes and in the public struggle over policies and ideas.

We have to be willing to jump into the fray, promoting ourselves, advancing our ideas, and tooting our own horns. Good stories will often carry the day.

My story is I am a direct descendant of Betsy Ross and of the first head coach of the Green Bay Packers of the National Football League. I have learned some lessons from the stories of my forebears that may help in the fight for the progressive center.

Betsy Ross was the legendary designer and maker of the first United States flag, and she was my great, great, great, great grandmother.

As my mother would have been proud to tell you, Betsy Griscom Ross Ashburn (first husband John Ross died in January 1776, second husband Joseph Ashburn died on March 3, 1782) married John Claypoole on May 8, 1783. Their daughter Jane married Caleb Canby. Their daughter Catherine married Lloyd Balderston. Their son William married Stella Sain. Their son William II married Susan Ramsay. Their daughter Eleanore married Joseph Hoeffel. I am their son.

I have never made a big deal in my political career about my direct relationship to Betsy Ross. It always seemed too self-promotional, and the few times I mentioned it to people I really do not think they believed me.

The one time I tried to capitalize on my relationship with Grandmother Betsy was at the Democratic National Convention in Chicago in 1996. I was running for Congress that year and attended a press conference organized by the Democratic Congressional Campaign Committee to give congressional challengers from around the country some national exposure. I knew I had to come up with something good to grab some attention from the crowded field of fellow candidates, so I trotted out the Betsy Ross connection.

None of the national reporters seemed to give a damn. The gambit fell flat during the press conference. But one reporter came up to me afterwards and asked me what I thought about the practice of flag burn-ing as a modern day protest. Unbelievably, I didn't get the connection and totally muffed the opportunity. Forgetting all about Grandmother Betsy, I gave the reporter an earnest, predictably liberal response about the im-portance of the First Amendment which protects free speech, no matter how odious, and so on. The reporter quickly lost interest and wandered away. My wife was incredulous and wondered why, if I was going to shame-lessly brag about Betsy Ross, I did not even try to connect her story and my relationship to her to the reporter's question about flag burning.

I had no good answer. I had no defense. I had blown the opportunity, and I haven't publicly talked about Grandmother Betsy since, until now.

I am also the grandson of the first coach of the NFL Green Bay Packers professional football team. My grandfather Joseph M. Hoeffel, according to contemporary newspaper reports in the *Green Bay Press-Gazette*,[1] was the head coach of the Packers in 1921, the first year the National Football League was organized.

Grandfather Hoeffel had been a football hero at the University of Wis-consin in 1912, captaining the team to an undefeated season and winning selection as second team All-American end. After graduation, he spent three years as an assistant football coach at the University of Nebraska. He returned to his hometown of Green Bay in 1916 to coach football at his alma mater, Green Bay East High School, where one of his players was Earl "Curly" Lambeau. Lambeau, of course, went on to Packer immortality as player, coach, and guiding spirit of the team and franchise. The official Packers website lists Lambeau as head coach from the semi-pro days of 1919 until 1949.

But who was head coach in 1921? Well, numerous news stories that fall season in the *Green Bay Press-Gazette* listed and quoted Joe Hoeffel as the head coach of the Green Bay Packers in their first season in the NFL.

Headlines in the paper during the season included, "Joe Hoeffel Will Coach Packer Team,"[2] "Coach Hoeffel Orders Three Days of Practice,"[3] "Coach Hoeffel's Team Shows Big Improvement in Practice,"[4] and "Coach Hoeffel Holds Big Workout."[5]

And my grandfather knew how to give good quotes. He sounded like every other football coach has sounded over the last century.

Before a game with the Chicago Cardinals, "Coach Hoeffel" is quoted in the *Press-Gazette* saying that Chicago "will have to show a lot of class to beat us. The players are working together finely and I think that we will show the Chicago fans a class of football which will surprise them."[6] Before a game with the Rock Island Independents "Coach Joe Hoeffel" said, "The Packers will be set for the foe. Rock Island has a wonderful team. But

I think we stand a good chance to give them a big surprise. We will have a machine out there Sunday, not alone individual stars."[7]

Grandfather reached the rhetorical heights of the 1921 football season when he was interviewed a few days before the big game with the Beloit Fairies that was billed as the professional football championship of Wisconsin. "Coach Hoeffel" predicted to the newspaper, "Well, there is one thing sure. Those Fairies are going to have their hands full Sunday afternoon and I think we are going to win."[8] You can't make up a quote like that.

The interesting part of this story is that my father never knew that his dad was the Packers first head coach in the NFL. Dad grew up in Green Bay, was close to his father and was a big pro football fan his entire life. But Grandfather Hoeffel simply never talked about his one-year stint as coach of the Packers. My dad knew that Grandfather was associated with the Packers in the early years, helping out his former high school player Curly Lambeau as the irrepressible Lambeau became the public face of pro football in Green Bay. Dad always thought that Grandfather had been a volunteer who helped out the Packers by coaching the line or the ends. But Dad always assumed, along with the rest of the football world, that Lambeau had been head coach as well as star player from the beginning.

The truth came to light due to the exhaustive research and excellent reporting of Cliff Christl, then a staff reporter for the Milwaukee Journal Sentinel and later the historian for the Packers. In well-documented articles in 2001, Christl uncovered the real identity of the first Packers' coach by wading through all of the stories written about the Packers in 1921 by the *Green Bay Press-Gazette*, as well as reviewing a number of other historical records.[9] Christl's reporting demonstrates that Joe Hoeffel was the first head coach of the NFL Green Bay Packers.

The Green Bay Packers were not pleased by this development at first. Although Christl's reporting forced the front office to acknowledge in interviews that the team's history was wrong, the Packers would not commit to changing the record book when the newspaper series was published in 2001. But later, the team acknowledged in the new Packers Hall of Fame the role my grandfather played. To their credit, the Packers want to get their history right, and they now understand that recognizing a former head coach like my grandfather does not in any way diminish the exploits and historic impact of the legendary Curly Lambeau.

So I have some notable forebears in Grandmother Betsy and Grandfather Hoeffel. What is really interesting is their stories are in a way mirror opposites. Grandfather really was the first coach of the Packers, but he didn't talk about it with his family or ever seek any credit, and recognition of his contributions has been slow to come. On the other hand, Grandmother Betsy, whom every school child believes designed and sewed the first United States flag, might not have done so at all. It turns out that the legend of Betsy Ross was actually first presented to the public by her own family nearly 50 years after her death, and nobody knows if it is true.

There is no question that Betsy Ross was an upholsterer and flag maker in Philadelphia during the American Revolution and for many years afterwards. In her excellent book *Betsy Ross and the Making of America*, Marla R. Miller documents that Grandmother Betsy was paid to make some sort of flag early on in the Revolutionary War, that her upholstery business made many flags for the Commonwealth of Pennsylvania and the United States, and her descendants continued in the flag-making business for several generations.[10]

But Miller points out that there is no documentation or proof that Grandmother designed or even sewed the first U.S. flag. Nobody knows who did. No proof exists for the legend that George Washington, George Ross, and Robert Morris visited Betsy Ross in mid-1776 as independence neared to discuss a new flag for the new nation, or that the Continental Congress requested her assistance, or that she demonstrated to Washington that a five pointed star would be far easier to mass produce than his favored six point star. No proof, just Grandmother Betsy's word for it.

It turns out that everything that connects Betsy Ross with the first flag comes from Betsy herself, as she proudly told the story in her retirement in the 1830s to her loving family. In turn, the Betsy Ross story was first presented to the public by her grandson William J. Canby in March 1870 in a paper he read to the Historical Society of Pennsylvania titled "The History of the Flag of the United States."[11]

Every word of the Betsy Ross legend may be true. After all, Grandmother Betsy was a sober, respected, and beloved figure among her family and friends. She was proud of the role she played during revolutionary times in Philadelphia and wanted to share her story with her family. But there are no letters, diary entries, or documents from any source that can prove the story. It all came from her and was promoted by her grandchildren.

So what does this dual family saga actually mean? For starters, it demonstrates the importance of family stories. Grandfather Hoeffel didn't brag about being the first head coach of the Packers and never told his son about it, so his well-documented story was almost lost to history but for the intrepid work of one newspaper reporter. Grandmother Betsy did share her story with her adoring family, and her descendants turned it into an enduring American legend, without any actual documents or proof.

The saga also demonstrates the power of a good story well told. The stuff of legends requires a storyline that makes sense and is pleasing to the listener. The United States after the Civil War was in need of healing, and when the Betsy Ross story was first presented in 1870, it struck a responsive chord in the hearts of many Americans who were in need of a unifying story. It certainly helped that the story starred a humble seamstress, who was the daughter, granddaughter, and great granddaughter of house carpenters, and also demonstrated that women too had important roles to play in our nation's founding.

Conversely, in Green Bay, Wisconsin, there is no need for myth building. The success of the Packers, and the legendary story of the team's founding heart and soul, Curly Lambeau, needs no embellishment. New discoveries of historic facts really won't complicate or confuse the legend. After all, in Green Bay, they don't play football on the frozen tundra of Hoeffel Field.

Progressives must take heart. We must fight back against the mythmaking of the other political side in America. We must understand the need to tell our story well, with straight talk and truth telling, based upon sound proposals that are both socially liberal and fiscally responsible.

We must have faith that the American people want a government that responds to the needs of the least, the last and the lost among us, while creating opportunity for all. We must believe in ourselves to promote a government that asks everyone to sacrifice a little in order for everyone to benefit a lot. We must fight to balance our budget through a reasonable program of careful belt tightening that protects those with the lowest incomes matched with progressive taxation that requires all to pay their fair share. We must fight for policies that improve the quality of life for all Americans.

This is the way to the progressive center in American politics. This is the way to come to grips with the Age of Trump. This is the way to win public support and win elections.

From the night of my first election in 1976, when I shadowboxed in the moonlight, I was totally enamored with politics and public service, and all these years later I still am. The world has gotten in a few licks of its own and evened up the score a bit, but I am still ahead on points and have enjoyed every minute of my public career.

Public service is the most honorable calling one can answer. It is the finest way to serve your community and your country. Public service is noble, and its nobility is not diminished because some politicians are not worthy.

My dad was always very proud of me and of my accomplishments in public life but never was entirely comfortable with all of the baggage that comes with politics. He would say to his friends in my presence, "My son has gone into government service," making it sound like we were a family of English aristocrats whose sons typically went into the Church, the Army, or the government.

I would protest, "Dad, I am a politician. It is OK to call me that." He would groan and his friends would laugh and we would go back to talking about anything but politics.

So the old question recurs: What the hell is going on here? Are politics and the political process able to help us figure out the answers to our national challenges, and then help us meet those challenges?

I believe that politics and the political process are the *only* way to figure out the answers and meet the challenges. Politics offers the opportunity to collectively resolve problems and create opportunities after all voices and opinions have been heard. Not all opinions will be heeded, but all should be heard. The give and take of politics is the best place I know to sort through the ideas we must choose and the decisions we must make to move all Americans forward.

So where do we go from here? It is certainly no time for shadowboxing, no time for the old political games. We have serious challenges, and we need serious proposals from serious politicians.

We need elected officials at all levels of government to think strategically and long term. The American preacher and author James Freeman Clarke said it best, "A politician . . . is a man who thinks of the next election; while a statesman thinks of the next generation."[12] My father quoted that one to me all the time. He surely was hoping it would sink in.

Progressives need to step up. The battle of political ideas is underway which will determine the future of our country. This is the time to fight for our beliefs, to promote the socially liberal, fiscally responsible policies that will allow us to balance the federal budget and invest in the American people.

The fundamental tenets of progressive liberalism are that we are all in this together, we need shared sacrifice to overcome the challenges that face us, we need to focus on the common good, and we need to embrace public action for the public good.

We agree with our conservative friends that nothing is more important to Americans than our individual freedom.

But progressives also know that we cannot enjoy that freedom if economic inequalities keep millions of us out of work or unfairly paid or uninsured. We cannot enjoy that freedom if we turn our backs on our international commitments and democratic alliances. We cannot be free if we shut our doors to immigrants based upon their religion or deny refugees the safety of our democracy. We cannot be free when unregulated corporations despoil our environment. We cannot be free when greedy bankers and reckless traders trash our pensions and vaporize our life savings. We cannot be free when our system of public education does not provide a good school for every neighborhood and every child. We cannot be free when some of us are disrespected, disadvantaged, and discriminated against simply because of our race, gender, sexual orientation, or home country. We cannot be free unless all have equal opportunity.

Winston Churchill, the English prime minister, is my number one all-time hero for his courage, steadfastness, and bold leadership that rallied an isolated England in 1940 and led to Hitler's defeat in World War II, and also for his stirring speeches and prolific writing.

Churchill was the rare politician with the intelligence to understand the big challenges, the courage to face them with toughness and resolve, the eloquence to inspire his countrymen to join him in the fight, and the literary skill to write about the victory, casting himself in the best possible light. Churchill was the whole package.

Before Winston Churchill was the leader of the Conservative Party and the wartime prime minister of England in the 1940s, he was a progressive liberal member of Parliament from 1904 to 1924. During that period of his long career he supported free trade and liberal reforms in Great Britain. He helped draft the legislation that created the first minimum wage and first unemployment pensions. He created labor exchanges to help the unemployed find jobs. He supported the "People's Budget" of 1909 that levied new taxes on the wealthy to pay for new social welfare programs, while opposing excessive Naval spending requests.

On October 11, 1906, in Glasgow, Scotland, Churchill delivered a speech offering a broad and humane vision for the future according to his official biographer Martin Gilbert, who quotes Churchill as follows:

> I do not want to see impaired the vigor of competition, but we can do much to mitigate the consequences of failure. We want to draw a line below which we will not allow persons to live and labor, yet above which they may compete with all the strength of their manhood. We want to have free competition upwards; we decline to allow free competition to run downwards. We do not want to pull down the structures of science and civilization, but to spread a net over the abyss.[13]

Churchill's vision embraced the value of competition and freedom for the average British laborer, as well as the need to protect that worker from the dire consequences of unfettered market forces. He believed that society should take public action for public good, encouraging vigorous efforts at self-improvement, while protecting against abject failure. He also made what likely is the first reference to what we now call the "social safety net" that most Americans support: a commitment from their government to provide for the disadvantaged through compassionate social programs and effective regulation of the private sector.

Donald Trump has brought a darker vision to today's America. The Age of Trump embraces a divisive approach that plays one group against another and demonizes opponents and critics. New domestic confrontations imperil workers, students, immigrants, the elderly, and the poor. New isolationism threatens our interests abroad and our safety at home.

Churchill's vision of a century ago still shines brightly today and offers a better way forward than the nastiness of the Age of Trump. Now, as then, we have an obligation to support the vulnerable among us while we provide opportunities for everyone to flourish and grow. Now, as then, we have an obligation to protect all citizens from falling through a shredded social safety net. Now, as then, we must husband our resources wisely to win public support for our agenda and to sustain our commitment to improving the quality of life for every American.

We understand the importance of investing in people while balancing the budget. We oppose the right-wing approach of "starving the beast," which simply cuts taxes and shrinks government. Bill Clinton showed us how to balance budgets with modest tax increases and prudent spending cuts. We must fight for the budget balance we need: Everybody pays a little and everybody sacrifices a little so everybody benefits a lot.

We recognize the danger of President Trump's "America First" policies that will overturn long-standing bipartisan national agreement on the wisdom of mutual defense agreements, democratic alliances, and open commerce between countries. We will strengthen ties with Western Europe to deter Russian expansionism, oppose bigoted immigration policies, and demand fair trade agreements that promote labor, environmental, and human rights standards. If Trump creates a Muslim registry, then we all will register as Muslims.

We know it is time to balance our budget. Two fiscal commissions have shown us how to reduce deficits, increase and stabilize revenues, and balance the federal budget fairly. We must embrace parity between spending cuts and tax increases, share the financial sacrifice among all players and all income levels, focus tax increases on higher incomes, protect the lowest incomes from deep spending cuts, and restore pay-as-you-go budget rules.

We have the courage of our convictions and will defend our principles and fight back against right-wing demonization. We are strong on national security, value bipartisan foreign policy, and will uphold religious tolerance. We will grow the economic pie for working families and also for the least, the last and the lost among us. Progressives will trust women to make their own reproductive decisions, support gun safety proposals and defend gay rights and marriage equality. We will fight for our beliefs, and the people will know where we stand.

We know we need more health-care reform, not less, that establishes Medicare for All. Right-wingers are foolishly demolishing Obamacare with no adequate replacement. We want single payer health insurance, where everyone is covered and everyone pays, medical providers are held responsible for the quality of their care, no discrimination in coverage is permitted, simplified administration and universal budgeting reduces financial waste, and public health is emphasized through prevention and strong primary care.

We believe it is time to fix our broken politics. The constant demands of campaign fund-raising challenge the integrity of politics and government. We must eliminate the abuses of gerrymandering and champion three reforms: more government transparency, no more no-bid contracts, and expanded public financing of elections.

We need big plans for our big country to restore economic strength and create jobs, to improve public schools, and to build stronger communities. We want to invest in new jobs and improved infrastructure. We want to grow our neighborhoods by coordinating spending on transportation, economic development, open space preservation, and community revitalization.

We know we need to "bring it" every day. We must connect with people in every way: from shaking hands to mastering media relations to using the five basics of making a persuasive speech. We need to understand the importance of looking voters in the eye and fighting for things that are meaningful to them, their families, and their futures. We need to stay in touch with our working class roots.

Let us fight for our socially liberal, fiscally responsible agenda in the public marketplace of ideas. Let us stand for balancing the budget and investing in people. Let us spread the net over the abyss. Let us move to the progressive center in American politics and government, and let us be smart enough to bring the people along with us.

Let us fight the Age of Trump. Let us find and hold the progressive center and get good things done for the American people.

Notes

Introduction

1. Thomas Sowell, "Finest Hour 163," International Churchill Society (Summer 2014).

Chapter One: Invest in People

1. U.S. Census Bureau press release, "Census Bureau Reports Congressional Voting Turnout Is at Lowest Mark Since 1978," July 16, 2015. For more information, see U.S. Census Bureau, "Current Population Survey, November 1978–2014." http://www.census .gov/hhes/www/socdemo/voting/.

2. William Butler Yeats, "Michael Robartes and the Dancer," William Harmon, ed., *The Classic Hundred Poems* (New York: Columbia University Press, 1998).

3. Frank Newport, "Americans Strongly Desire That Political Leaders Work Together," The Gallup Poll, January 19, 2011.

4. Grover Norquist, interview on NPR's "Morning Edition," May 25, 2001.

5. Robert T. Mann, *Legacy to Power: Senator Russell Long of Louisiana* (iUniverse: 2003), 333.

6. Kenneth T. Walsh, "George W. Bush's 'Bullhorn' Moment," U.S. News, April 25, 2013.

7. George W. Bush, conversation with author on Air Force One, flight from Philadelphia to Washington, DC, March 2002.

8. Kathy Ruffing and Joel Friedman, "Economic Downturn and Legacy of Bush Policies Continue to Drive Large Deficits," Center for Budget and Policy Priorities, February 28, 2013.

9. Sarah Palin, NPR's "Weekend Edition Sunday," February 7, 2010.

10. Aimee Picchi, CBS News "Moneywatch," March 16, 2015.

11. https://www.treasurydirect.gov/govt/reports/pd/mspd/mspd.htm.

12. http://www.ontheissues.org/Celeb/Dick_Cheney_Budget_+_Economy.htm.

13. Conversation between Israeli mother and author, West Bank, Palestinian territories, October 1983.

Chapter Two: America First

1. Victor Chernomyrdin, conversation with author, Moscow, Russia, February 2001.
2. Adam Taylor and Michael Birnbaum, "Baltic States Respond to Trump Jibe," *Philadelphia Inquirer*, July 22, 2016, A17.
3. Lawrence J. Haas, *Harry & Arthur: Truman, Vandenberg, and the Partnership That Created the Free World* (Lincoln, NE: Potomac Books, University of Nebraska Press, 2016), 253.
4. 50 U.S.C. Sections 1541–48.
5. Peter Baker, "Obama's Duel View of War Power Seeks Limits and Leeway," *New York Times*, February 11, 2015.
6. Susan Davis, "Senators Press Administration on Need for AUMF Vote," *USA Today*, March 11, 2015.

Chapter Three: Balance the Budget

1. Alan Fram, "GOP's Ban on Earmarks Far from Airtight," *Philadelphia Inquirer*, November 10, 2010, A2.
2. "All about Pork: The History, Abuse and Future of Earmarks," Citizens against Government Waste, November 2015.
3. https://www.fiscalcommission.gov.
4. https://www.fiscalcommission.gov/sites/fiscalcommission.gov/files/documents/The MomentofTruth12–1–2010.pdf. (p. 10).
5. Ibid., 11.
6. https://bipartisanpolicy.org/wp-content/uploads/sites/default/files/BPC.
7. David Leonhardt and Bill Marsh, "Get a Pencil. You're Tackling the Deficit." *New York Times*, November 14, 2010, 4.
8. http://www.truthdig.com/report/item/20090723_the_attack_of_the_1-percenters.
9. Mark Zandi, "Our Fiscal Challenges Are Big, but Manageable," *Philadelphia Inquirer*, November 28, 2010.
10. http://www.fixthedebt.org/5-ways-washington-can-make-good-on-promises-to-fix-the-debt.

Chapter Four: Courage of Our Convictions

1. http://www.politico.com/story/2010/08/obama-defends-ground-zero-mosque-041060.
2. Edward Wyatt, "3 Republicans Criticize Obama's Endorsement of Mosque," *New York Times*, August 14, 2010.
3. Ibid.
4. Ibid.
5. Ibid.
6. David Seifman, "Bloomberg Defends Ground Zero Mosque as Freedom-of-Faith Issue," *New York Post*, May 29, 2010.
7. https://georgewbush-whitehouse.archives.gov/news/releases/2001/09/20010917–11 .html.

8. Jenna Johnson, "Trump Calls for 'Total and Complete Shutdown of Muslims Entering the United States,'" *Washington Post*, December 7, 2015.

9. https://www.loc.gov/lcib/9806/danbury.html.

10. *Roe v. Wade*, 410 U.S. 113 (1973)

11. William Ecenberger, "The Life and Death of Senate Bill 742," *Philadelphia Inquirer, Today Magazine*, January 31, 1982, 16–18.

12. Ibid.

13. Ibid.

14. Ibid.

15. http://openjurist.org/737/f2d/283/american-college-of-obstetricians-and-gynecologists-pennsylvania-section-v-thornburgh.

16. Carolyn McCarthy, Congressional Record (June 17, 1999), H4605.

17. Roll Call 235, Congressional Record (June 17, 1999), H4605.

18. "Sarah Palin Steps Up the Rhetoric against Her Detractors," *Associated Press*, March 29, 2010.

19. http://everytown.org/.

20. Robert Alan Goldberg, *Barry Goldwater* (New Haven, CT: Yale University Press, 1997), 332.

21. Barry M. Goldwater, "The Gay Ban: Just Plain Un-American," *Washington Post*, June 10, 1993.

22. Lloyd Grove, "Barry Goldwater's Left Turn," *Washington Post*, July 28, 1994, C01.

23. Ibid.

24. Ariane de Vogue and Jeremy Diamond, "Supreme Court Rules in Favor of Same-Sex Marriage Nationwide," CNN, June 27, 2015.

25. Darren K. Carlson, "Public OK with Gays, Women in Military," Gallup Poll, December 23, 2003.

26. "Obama Signs Hate Crimes Bill into Law," CNN, October 28, 2009.

27. http://www.americanrhetoric.com/speeches/mlktempleisraelhollywood.htm.

28. http://quoteinvestigator.com/2015/03/30/passion/.

Chapter Five: Medicare for All

1. Glenn Kessler, "Sarah Palin, 'Death Panels' and 'Obamacare,'" *Washington Post*, June 27, 2012.

2. Robert A. Caro, *The Years of Lyndon Johnson: Master of the Senate* (New York: Knopf, 1994), 120.

3. Kimball Payne, "Cuccinelli Compliments Ruling Supporting Health Care Reform," *Newport News, VA Daily Press*, February 23, 2011.

4. "Women's Suffrage and Other Visions of Right-Wing Apocalypse," The New Republic, December 21, 2009. (Compiled by Benjamin Bernstein, Benjamin Birnbaum, Lydia DePillis, Noah Kristula-Green, Amanda Silverman, Julie Sobel and Jesse Zwick.)

5. *National Federation of Independent Business v. Sebelius*, 567 U.S. (2012), 11–393.

6. Ibid.

7. https://www.healthcare.gov/.

8. https://www.opensecrets.org/industries/summary/.

9. Lisa Potetz, Health Policy Alternatives, and Juliette Cubanski and Tricia Neuman, Kaiser Family Foundation, "Medicare Spending and Financing: A Primer," Kaiser Family Foundation, February 2011.

10. Robert Pear, "A Battle to Change Medicare Is Brewing, Whether Trump Wants It or Not," *New York Times*, November 24, 2016.

11. Steffie Woolhandler, M. D., M.P.H., Terry Campbell, M.H.A., and David U. Himmelstein, M. D., "Costs of Health Care Administration in the United States and Canada," *New England Journal of Medicine*, August 21, 2003.

12. https://www.oecd.org/health/healthsystems/Focus-Health-Spending-2015.pdf.

Chapter Six: It's Broke—So Fix It

1. Nate Cohn, "Blaming Gerrymandering Has Its Limits, as Pennsylvania Shows," *New York Times*, September 8, 2014. Also, Sean Trende, "In Pennsylvania, the Gerrymander of the Decade?" RealClearPolitics, December 14, 2011.

2. Bernard Grofman, "The Supreme Court Will Examine Partisan Gerrymandering in 2017. That Could Change the Voting Map," *Washington Post*, January 31, 2017.

3. John Emerich Edward Dalberg Acton, first Baron Acton, letter to Bishop Mandell Creighton, 1887.

4. Pennsylvania Sunshine Act, 65 Pa.C.S. Sections 701–716.

5. Stan Huskey, "Waiting for the Pin to Drop," *Norristown Times Herald,* Editorial, March 3, 2011.

6. Michael C. Jensen, "Nixon Drive May Have Got 15 Illegal Corporate Gifts," *New York Times*, August 24, 1973, 1.

7. *Citizens United v. Federal Election Commission* 558 U.S. 50 (2010).

8. E.J. Dionne, "2010 Class War Fought in the Shadows," *Columbia Daily Tribune*, October 13, 2010.

9. Jeff Zeleny, "Political Fallout from the Supreme Court Ruling," *New York Times*, January 21, 2010.

10. Deborah Tedford, "Supreme Court Rips Up Campaign Finance Laws," NPR, January 21, 2010.

11. S. 1538, 114th Congress (2015–2016).

12. H.R. 1826, 111th Congress (2009–2010).

Chapter Seven: No Little Plans

1. Charles Moore, *Daniel Burnham, Architect, Planner of Cities, Vol. 2* (New York: Houghton Mifflin, 1921), 147.

2. http://www.china.org.cn/english/government/207279.htm.

3. https://www.cartercenter.org/documents/541.html#2.

4. No Child Left Behind Act of 2001, Pub. L. 107–110, 115 Stat.1425, enacted January 8, 2002, repealed December 10, 2015.

5. https://www2.ed.gov/programs/racetothetop/executive-summary.pdf.

6. David Arsen and Yongmei Ni, "The Competitive Effect of School Choice Policies on Performance in Traditional Public Schools," National Education Policy Center, March 1, 2008.

7. Ed Rendell, "Trade Equals Jobs," *Pittsburgh Post-Gazette*, March 16, 2015.

8. http://www.pepperlaw.com/publications/governor-edward-g-rendell-signs-the-alter native-energy-investment-act-2008-07-31/.

9. http://sbecouncil.org/about-us/facts-and-data/.

10. http://www.montcopa.org/638/Open-Space-Program.

11. http://www.montcopa.org/ArchiveCenter/ViewFile/Item/552.

12. http://econsultsolutions.com/wp-content/uploads/2013/06/Montgomery-County-Final-Report-With-Appendices-12.5.08.pdf.

Chapter Eight: Bring It Every Day

1. William J. Clinton, conversation with James Maza, Onorato for Governor rally, Carver Community Center, Norristown, Pennsylvania, October 28, 2010.

2. Daylin Leach, conversation with author, Sestak for Senate rally, Bryn Mawr, Pennsylvania, October 28, 2010.

3. William J. Clinton, conversation with author at Hillary Clinton rally, North Penn High School, Lansdale, Pennsylvania, April 2008.

4. http://reagan2020.us/speeches/City_Upon_a_Hill.asp.

5. Alex Markels, "George H. W. Bush Checks His Watch during Debate with Bill Clinton and Ross Perot," *U.S. News*, January 17, 2008.

6. Charles P. Pierce, "Tip O'Neill's Idea That All Politics Is Local Is How Government Dies," *Esquire*, July 17, 2015.

7. http://www.sheehanassociates.com/cs/bios/michael_sheehan.

8. Brett and Kate McKay, "The Winston Churchill Guide to Public Speaking," *The Art of Manliness*, May 28, 2015.

Conclusion

1. Cliff Christl, "A Leap in Lambeau's History: Hoeffel Coached Packers When They Joined League in 1921, Records Reveal," *Milwaukee Journal Sentinel*, October 28, 2001, A1.

2. *Green Bay Press-Gazette*, September 10, 1921.

3. Ibid., October 20, 1921.

4. Ibid., November 4, 1921.

5. Ibid., November 18, 1921.

6. Ibid., November 17, 1921.

7. Ibid., October 27, 1921.

8. Ibid., October 14, 1921.

9. Christl, "A Leap in Lambeau's History," A1, A10.

10. Marla R. Miller, *Betsy Ross and the Making of America* (New York: Henry Holt, 2010).

11. http://www.ushistory.org/betsy/more/canby.htm.

12. James Freeman Clarke, *Old and New, Volume II* (Boston: Roberts Brothers, 1870), 664.

13. Martin Gilbert, *Churchill: A Life* (New York: Holt, 1992), 183–184.

Index

About the Author

Joseph M. Hoeffel is a veteran advocate for progressive public policies and good government in Pennsylvania and the country. For 25 years, he served in elected office as a three-term United States Congressman, four-term Pennsylvania State Representative, and three-term Montgomery County Commissioner. Joe believes in robust public action for the public good and supported socially liberal and fiscally responsible policies. Hoeffel started "Iraq Watch" to advocate through House debate for changes in our military and foreign policies in Iraq, and he proposed a modern-day Marshall Plan for economic revitalization in the Middle East and Eurasia. He is a graduate of Boston University and Temple University School of Law. Joe and his wife Francesca live in Abington, Pennsylvania.